ORTHO'S All About

The Easiest Flowers To Grow

Written by Penelope O'Sullivan
Photographed by Jerry Pavia

Meredith® Books
Des Moines, Iowa

Ortho® Books
An imprint of Meredith® Books

All About the Easiest Flowers to Grow
Editor: Michael McKinley
Contributing Technical Editors: Dr. Steven Still,
   Ohio State University; Stephanie Cohen
Art Director: Tom Wegner
Assistant Art Director: Harijs Priekulis
Copy Chief: Catherine Hamrick
Copy and Production Editor: Terri Fredrickson
Book Production Managers: Pam Kvitne,
   Marjorie J. Schenkelberg
Contributing Copy Editor: Barbara Feller-Roth
Technical Proofreader: Fran Gardner
Contributing Proofreaders: Mary Duerson,
   Kathy Roth Eastman, Beth Lastine, Elizabeth Neils,
   Barbara J. Stokes
Contributing Illustrator: Mike Eagleton
Contributing Map Illustrator: Jana Fothergill
Indexer: Donald Glassman
Electronic Production Coordinator: Paula Forest
Editorial and Design Assistants: Kathleen Stevens,
   Karen Schirm

Additional Editorial Contributions from
   Art Rep Services
Director: Chip Nadeau
Designer: lk Design

Meredith® Books
Editor in Chief: James D. Blume
Design Director: Matt Strelecki
Managing Editor: Gregory H. Kayko
Executive Ortho Editor: Larry Erickson

Director, Retail Sales and Marketing: Terry Unsworth
Director, Sales, Special Markets: Rita McMullen
Director, Sales, Premiums: Michael A. Peterson
Director, Sales, Retail: Tom Wierzbicki
Director, Sales, Home & Garden Centers: Ray Wolf
Director, Book Marketing: Brad Elmitt
Director, Operations: George A. Susral
Director, Production: Douglas M. Johnston

Vice President, General Manager: Jamie L. Martin

Meredith Publishing Group
President, Publishing Group: Christopher M. Little
Vice President, Finance & Administration: Max Runciman

Meredith Corporation
Chairman and Chief Executive Officer: William T. Kerr

Chairman of the Executive Committee: E.T. Meredith III

Thanks to
Spectrum Communication Services, Inc.

Additional Photography by:
   (Photographers credited may retain copyright ©
   to the listed photographs.)
L = Left, R = Right, C = Center, B = Bottom, T = Top
Ernie Braun: 15R
Josephine Coatsworth: 41, 73C
Steve Cridland: 11B
Derek Fell: 38BL, 39BL, 39BR, 77C
David Goldberg: 36, 37, 38C, 39CB, 43, 45L
Jerry Howard/Positive Images: 38BR, 45R
Mike Jensen: 34
Balthazar Korab: 4, 9B
Pete Krumhardt: 13TR
Kathy Longinaker: 39T
Bryan McCay: 35, 44R
Michael McKinley: 58C
Mary Pindar: 5
Nancy Rotenberg: 61B
Eric Roth: 11T
Julie Semel: 10
Maris/Semel: 13TL, 32
David Toht: 39CT

On the cover: Black-eyed Susan (*Rudbeckia fulgida* var. *deamii*) and Italian aster (*Aster amellus* 'King George') are two foolproof flowers that provide months of late-season color. Photograph by Andrew Lawson.

All of us at Ortho® Books are dedicated to providing you with the information and ideas you need to enhance your home and garden. We welcome your comments and suggestions about this book. Write to us at:
   Meredith Corporation
   Ortho Books
   1716 Locust St.
   Des Moines, IA 50309–3023

If you would like more information on other Ortho products, call 800-225-2883 or visit us at www.ortho.com

Note to the Readers: Due to differing conditions, tools, and individual skills, Meredith Corporation assumes no responsibility for any damages, injuries suffered, or losses incurred as a result of following the information published in this book. Before beginning any project, review the instructions carefully, and if any doubts or questions remain, consult local experts or authorities. Because codes and regulations vary greatly, you always should check with authorities to ensure that your project complies with all applicable local codes and regulations. Always read and observe all of the safety precautions provided by manufacturers of any tools, equipment, or supplies, and follow all accepted safety procedures.

FLOWERS ARE FUN

Lavish flower borders are easy to grow when you choose plants appropriate to your site. In this sunny northern garden, daisies, daylilies, Asiatic lilies, delphiniums, feverfew, and baby's breath transform a modest house into a lavish wonderland. The well-tended garden makes the entire property appear tidy and in excellent condition.

Easy flowers work magic in the garden. With little effort, you can use them to enhance the landscape, adding verve, color, and style to a plain house, and charm and elegance to a fashionable one. Easy flowers are sturdy and healthy, and long-blooming. They're often familiar and easy to find. They weave in and out of memory with rich associations—violets plucked from the lawn in spring, lilacs scenting the front path, thorny roses pricking fingertips when grabbed and sniffed. The sweet, spicy fragrance of old-fashioned flowering tobacco and Oriental lilies draws you to the window on warm, humid nights. Cheery orange zinnias and true-blue flossflowers lift the spirit; blooms in harmonious pastels soothe the soul. Flowers can change space. They improve ugly fences and create private places. Choose the right plants for the conditions of your site, and they'll reward you with bountiful blossoms that brighten your home indoors and out.

BENEFITS OF EASY FLOWERS

CURB APPEAL: Attractive plantings of easy flowers add value to your house. Vivid flowers draw attention away from flaws and give you an opportunity to express yourself through form, color, and fragrance.

QUALITY OF LIFE: Flowers bring beauty to the environment and pleasure to those who see them.

BIG BANG FOR THE BUCK: Within six weeks, the annuals you buy in six-packs can fill a flower bed. Perennials add color and form to your garden for years and years.

FLOWERS WITHOUT FUSS: Your green thumb will show when you raise long-blooming flowers that suit your site and require little care.

READY SUPPLY OF CUT FLOWERS: Many annuals bloom longest and best when you cut them regularly. The more you delight your friends and family with bountiful bouquets, the more flowers your plants will produce.

BEAUTIFUL WILDLIFE: Bees, birds, and butterflies add sound, motion, and liveliness to the flower garden. Giving birds and beneficial insects food and shelter encourages them to stay close and help control insect pests in your yard.

INTERESTING SPACE: Flowers can define paths, direct foot traffic, and create walls of privacy and color.

RAPID EFFECT: Whereas shrubs and trees take years to mature, flowers fill space fast.

TIME TO ENJOY THE GARDEN INSTEAD OF WORKING IN IT: You deserve a rest. Gardening with easy flowers cuts your work to a minimum.

HOW TO USE THIS BOOK

This book is simple to use. At the beginning of each chapter, you'll find a brief overview of the contents. To start off, don't miss the next two pages of this introduction (pages 6–7), where we distill the essence of this book into the 12 secrets of easy flower gardening. In "Combining Flowers" (pages 8–15), you'll find a wealth of advice for designing a garden that provides maximum impact for the least effort. "16 Easy Flower Gardens" (pages 16–31) shows how to apply design principles by offering complete plans that you can adopt as is or use for ideas. "Easy Flowers: Planting and Care" (pages 32–45) explains the techniques of growing and maintaining flowers for the greatest success and minimum effort. The "Gallery of Easy Flowers" (pages 46–91) presents a handy bloom-season chart, an A–Z selection and growing guide for more than 100 of the easiest flowers, and a resource guide to finding special plants and seeds.

'Jacob Kline' bee balm, Chinese astilbe, butterfly bush, purple coneflower, and phlox—flowers loved by butterflies and hummingbirds—surround a fountain where birds splash in the hot summer sun. Purple coneflower is good for cutting, and it also produces seed heads that provide winter food for finches.

12 SECRETS OF EASY FLOWER GARDENING

Foxglove fills this sunny raised bed with warm pastel color. A biennial that self-sows freely, this plant produces a generous supply of cut flowers in late spring and early summer. Each bell-shaped bloom looks like an enchanted fairy hat.

FOLLOW THESE GUIDELINES TO ENSURE SUCCESS

1. KNOW WHAT YOU WANT. Before you buy a plant or dig a hole, figure out why you want a flower garden. Are you dressing up a foundation planting? Are you interested in attracting birds and butterflies? Do you want cut flowers all season long? Knowing your purpose saves time, money, and effort.

2. HAVE A PLAN. Half the fun is dreaming up a design just right for your home. Decide which hues look best with your house color, which plants will go where, and whether you should change the site before planting. If your project includes a deck, patio, or other structural feature, it's best to address those aspects of the garden before planting.

3. START SMALL. Be realistic about the size of your garden. Don't take on more than you can manage. Gardening does take time, especially in the beginning. Containers, for example, may require watering every day during the hottest days of summer. Start small and work in stages over several years to turn your whole lot into a wonderland of flowers.

4. CHOOSE HARDWORKING PLANTS. You expect your home to look good all year, so why not demand the same from your garden? Cultivate spring, summer, and fall flowers for a succession of blooms and multiseason appeal. Many annuals and a few perennials offer blooms over an extraordinarily long season. Most perennials produce flowers for a shorter period, but some provide more than one season of interest with flowers, fruit, fall color, and handsome foliage and form.

5. CHOOSE TOUGH PLANTS. Choose disease- and pest-resistant varieties to reduce fussing with pesticides and to ensure plant health. For example, although garden phlox and bee balm are susceptible to mildew, recent hybridization has created new disease-resistant varieties.

6. CHOOSE THE RIGHT PLANT FOR THE PLACE. Get to know your site first, then select plants that are naturally adapted to it. A lot of gardening work (and failure) stems from gardening backward—trying to fix a site after planting it with ill-suited plants. If you try to grow plants that aren't hardy in your area, you'll have to coddle them through every winter. Plant a rhododendron in full sun and alkaline soil, and you will continually struggle to rig up shade and apply soil acidifier for it to survive—if it ever does. Don't fight your site. Use plants adapted to growing there.

7. BEGIN WITH GOOD SOIL. Great flowers grow in great soil. Many people live with soil stripped of nutrients, robbed of oxygen, and compacted by heavy equipment during house-building. Test your soil to learn about its condition and what is necessary to improve it. You can accomplish gardening miracles by testing and amending your soil; nearly all soils can be improved by adding organic matter.

8. MULCH, MULCH, MULCH. Mulching garden beds has several advantages. Mulch on a flower bed cools the soil in summer, helping it stay moist. Mulch smothers weed seeds so most can't germinate; the ones that do are easier to pull. As organic mulches such as shredded bark decompose, they condition the soil by raising the level of organic matter. Mulched flowers also stay cleaner and healthier because less dirt splashes their petals when the plants are watered.

9. REGULAR MAINTENANCE IS EASY MAINTENANCE. Although mulched areas require less maintenance, flower beds still need watering, fertilizing, deadheading, and weeding to keep them in tip-top shape. Get in the habit of spending small amounts of time in the garden regularly to prevent chores from mounting up. Just five to ten minutes every morning can keep your garden fresh when others are filled with dead stems and faded flowers.

10. TREAT PROBLEMS WHEN THEY'RE SMALL. Problems caught early tend to go away fast. Weeds are a snap to pull when they're tiny seedlings but a major project to remove after they grow deep roots. Watering flowers before they're stressed with drought prevents damage that can allow other problems to develop. Catching a pest outbreak in its infancy can eliminate the need for time-consuming and costly intervention later. By dealing with problems fast, you can prevent serious damage from occurring.

11. WHEN IN DOUBT, RIP IT OUT. Keep your spade sharp! Sometimes a plant simply doesn't work. The color is wrong or the plant sickens and dies. If that's the case, be ruthless. Don't waste time babying plants that will not perform. Every gardener makes mistakes—gardening is trial-and-error. Move healthy plants that outgrow their space to a suitable new location. Pest- or disease-ridden plants that can't be saved belong in the trash. Remove plants you don't like and substitute others. Give the plants to friends who want them. Annuals and perennials are often inexpensive and easy to replace.

12. DON'T WORRY, BE HAPPY. For easy flower gardening, attitude is key. Relax! Delight in the loose edges, casual abundance, and growing surprises Mother Nature has in store for you—the chance seedling, the too-early bloom, the unexpected combination. If you strive for perfect neatness and rigid predictability, count on plenty of effort. The pleasant rough edges and happy accidents of nature are some of gardening's greatest gifts.

Tough, hardworking plants ensure maximum bloom with minimum fuss. Here, drifts of 'Moonbeam' coreopsis, pink coreopsis, Stokes' aster, and petunias flow into one another, creating a soothing tapestry of soft color.

COMBINING FLOWERS

Easy flowers provide maximum effect when you combine them well. This chapter shows how to do that by looking at aspects of garden design, including color, grouping, style, and composition. Knowing the garden's purpose helps you position it and can provide a unifying theme that makes plant choice easier. For example, if you live in an old house and have trouble mowing around a lamppost in the lawn, consider installing a Victorian-style formal island with some tender exotics and tropical plants around the post to make mowing easier. Your garden's physical conditions are also important when determining which plants will grow easily on your site. Purpose, climate, microclimates, soil type, and the amount and quality of sun and shade in your garden determine the best types of flowers for you to grow.

Above: 'Melody Red' pansies create a warm background for an attention-grabbing display of hot red-and-yellow 'Tubergen's Gem' tulips. Right: Masses of blue lithodora, purple Spanish bluebells, and white daphne combine with sprays of green leaves to form a restful tapestry of cool colors.

COLOR

Color choices affect the way a garden is perceived. When used thoughtfully, color has the power to harmonize, energize, evoke moods, or change space. Color is personal—there is no right or wrong. What's most important is to understand how color works and to use that knowledge to experiment and have some fun.

The three aspects of a color are *hue*, *value*, and *intensity*. As shown in the color wheel at right, blue, red, and yellow are the *primary hues*, and green, purple, and orange— each mixed from two of the primaries— are *secondary hues*. Red, orange, and yellow are warm hues that leap to the front of a visual composition. Blue, violet, and purple are cool and visually recede in a garden design.

Value refers to lightness and darkness based on a scale of black to white. Within the range of blue, for example, values range from dark to light. Powder blue is a *tint*, or light color; navy is a *shade*, or dark color.

Intensity indicates purity or saturation. A highly saturated color is strong and brilliant, whereas a color with low intensity is not bright but grayed.

Harmonious garden colors live side by side on the color wheel and share a similar value and intensity. For instance, the saturated reds, oranges, and yellows of late summer blend well in the garden, as do springtime tints of pink, purple, and blue.

Contrasting colors, known as *complements*, are opposites on the color wheel. Thus blue and orange, red and green, and yellow and purple form powerful pairs in the landscape, because each color makes its complement stand out, for maximum drama.

Light influences the way we see colors. At noon, sunlight bleaches color and throws bold shadows. Thus a flower garden around a swimming pool used mostly at midday benefits from colors of high saturation, whereas soft, misty morning light enhances delicate pinks, yellows, and blues.

White, green and gray are the important neutrals of the garden, essential for blending, highlighting, and serving as a background for other colors. When using neutrals, look for underlying tones of blue, red, or yellow. Cool-toned flowers and foliage soften a garden of blues or pastels, whereas warm tones enrich yellows, oranges, and reds.

Unifying your garden with color is easy when you plant shades and tints of one color to create a monochromatic theme. If the idea of an all-pink or all-purple garden isn't appealing, you can still bring unity to your garden by repeating a color throughout the design. This color can dominate some garden areas and in others provide either a contrasting accent or an echo of similar hue.

Opposites attract in this bold design based on the contrasting hues of golden barberry and violet-blue 'May Night' salvia. Use a color wheel to help plan for harmony and contrast.

EVENING COLORS

If you work indoors during the day and cannot venture outside until dusk, plant your garden with evening in mind. In the evening, dark colors disappear into shadows, but white and pale yellow flowers shine in moonlight's amber glow.

The royalty of the evening garden are the scented white flowers that bloom at night. A few plants of flowering tobacco perfume even a large garden with sweet spice, while its pendant white flowers, less noticeable by day, loom large at dusk. Moonflower, a fragrant, night-blooming vine, has 6-inch white flowers and, grown on a trellis, adds a vertical accent to the garden. Several yellow daylilies, including the heirloom 'Hyperion', are sweetly scented and flower at night.

GROUPING FLOWERS

Color is not the only factor to consider when designing a flower garden. Grouping plants by balancing their forms adds further richness to a plan. Some characteristics of a plant's form are shape or general outline, height, mass, spread, and texture. Mass refers to an object's visual weight and bulk. The mass of a plant is significant not just in relationship to other plant masses in the design but also to open space. Spread is a variable factor depending on the age and health of the plant. When you plan a garden, consider a plant's mature spread rather than its size when you buy it. Perennials often take three years to achieve a mature spread.

Plants range in texture from coarse to fine, and combining those textures well adds to the garden's charm. When considering a plant's texture, take both the flowers and the foliage into account. For perennials in particular, foliage is on view far longer than the flowers. For a harmonious look, combine coarser plants with plants of medium texture. At the same time, group medium-textured plants next to those with fine textures.

Grouping like flowers en masse makes a more powerful statement in the garden than displaying them singly. As in the army, there's strength in numbers, and a drift of daylilies possesses a far greater presence than one plant could ever have. For a natural effect, mass flowers in asymmetrical drifts flowing in and out of other flower groups. Use odd numbers of plants arranged densely in the middle and sparsely near the edges, as if you had broadcast seeds by hand.

Straight lines of flowers sometimes work in formal bedding schemes where distinctly formed color areas create a pattern. The cutting garden also benefits from straight rows because production of cut flowers is its goal. Straw-covered paths keep down weeds and provide easy access to cutting rows, giving this kind of garden a tidy, rustic appeal. In other gardens, however, a single plant with large, dramatic flowers, an imposing architectural form, or bold, colorful foliage can create a bold accent in an otherwise massed design.

This strongly defined summer border relies on masses of warm-colored daylilies and bee balm for its effect. The border's serpentine shape increases its dramatic impact, and its mixture of early-, mid-, and late-season daylilies ensures all-summer color.

COLOR ALL SEASON LONG

Gardens need to look good throughout the entire growing season. Thus an important strategy for an easy flower garden is grouping plants that prolong the period of bloom and create multiseasonal effects. Selecting plants requires thought, because each has a season of bloom ranging from a week or two to as long as several months. Many annuals bloom from spring to frost, giving you months of colorful garden flowers. A few perennial varieties have been bred for similarly long seasons of bloom. Moreover, you can extend the bloom of plants such as tulips, daylilies, peonies, poppies, irises, and daffodils by planting early-, mid-, and late-season varieties of each flower. Check the bloom chart in the "Gallery of Easy Flowers" (pages 48–49) to see the range of bloom for specific flowers and to choose combinations for extended interest.

Certain planting techniques help ensure flowers throughout the season. Stagger plants to take advantage of their seasons of bloom. For example, instead of placing all spring-flowering perennials side by side, alternate them with later-blooming perennials for a garden that keeps on blooming. If the same plants appear in different places throughout the garden, the repetition also increases the garden's unity.

Interplant flowers with different seasons of bloom. For example, plant a sequence of early-, mid-, and late-season daffodil varieties that bloom in succession from March through May. To hide their unsightly yellowing foliage, which remains for months after the daffodils have faded, you can interplant early-, mid-, and late-season daylilies with the daffodil bulbs; the emerging leaves of the daylilies will hide the fading foliage of the daffodils. (For the daffodils' health, you should neither cut, braid, nor tie with rubber bands the unsightly leaves.) By June, the daylilies will have already closed the gap and begun their summer-long show.

Learn to cultivate plants not just for their flowers but for other attributes. Many plants, such as coleus and caladium, sport foliage as colorful as any flower and much longer-lasting in effect. Other plants, such as ornamental pepper and purple hyacinth bean, bear attractive, edible fruit that extends the season of interest. Black-eyed Susan, purple coneflower, 'Autumn Joy' sedum, and Joe-Pye weed all produce attractive seed heads that are an asset in the garden from fall well into winter. And a few plants, such as blue plumbago, hardy geraniums, amsonia and Solomon's seal, as well as many ornamental grasses, even provide outstanding fall foliage color in brilliant red, bronze, or yellow.

TOP 10 LONG-BLOOMING PERENNIALS

'Moonbeam' threadleaf coreopsis
'Luxuriant' fringed bleeding heart
Purple coneflower
Blanket flower
False sunflower
Russian sage
'Goldsturm' black-eyed Susan
'Butterfly Blue' pincushion flower
'Autumn Joy' sedum
'Homestead Purple' verbena

Pansies, which flourish in spring and fall, grow in the window box along with nasturtiums, which bloom from summer to frost. Beneath the window box, impatiens finds the perfect shaded conditions for abundant growth.

Russian sage, 'Goldsturm' black-eyed Susan, and 'Autumn Joy' sedum provide months of color midsummer to fall. They combine well with the fine textures of grasses.

PUTTING IT ALL TOGETHER

The purpose of your flower garden and your expectations define its limits. A cheerful entry garden with a nicely landscaped front path is visible to friends and strangers alike. A meditation garden, on the other hand, requires privacy. If you can't find a spot to be alone on your property, you can create one with plants and building materials.

Other gardens are based on practical considerations. An outdoor dining room should be close to the house for easy access to the kitchen. To create views from indoors, determine where you like to sit or stand when looking outside and plant your vistas accordingly. Flower beds sometimes protect trees in the lawn from lawn mower damage and make for easy mowing around lampposts. With these pragmatic plantings, you also beautify your property and save precious time for other tasks.

Right: Informal plantings of evening primrose, fleabane, rosemary, and lavender flank a curving stone path. The blue gate and pink path harmonize with the soft pinks and blues of the flowers. Below: A weathered bench nestles among brilliant garden flowers as a haven for tired gardeners.

FLOWER GARDEN TYPES

The kind of garden you choose determines its shape and placement on your lot. Flower borders create colorful edges along driveways, hedges, walls, fences, and paths. Herbaceous borders contain plants with nonwoody stems, such as annuals, perennials, and bulbs. Mixed borders, on the other hand, may include perennials, annuals, bulbs, vines, ornamental shrubs, and small trees. A well-designed border works as a cohesive whole rather than a jumble of disconnected parts. Repeated forms and colors and balanced masses bring unity to border designs.

Flower beds can be geometric or flowing in shape. They're usually meant to be seen close up. Beds lining patios, decks, and house foundations work best when planted for season-long interest.

In addition to protecting trees and making it easier to mow around lampposts, island beds add drama to the landscape. Brightly colored impatiens massed beneath a small tree and seen from afar create a focal point in a large lawn. In urban settings, paving instead of lawn may surround geometrical islands of ornamental grasses, flowers, and shrubs, creating an approachable oasis of natural forms and colors in a sea of gray.

STYLE

Style reflects a garden's mood. Formal gardens are architectural, extending the rooms of the house they surround. A line drawn from a front or back door to a distant bench or an urn can become the main axis of a formal garden. The simple formal garden has symmetrical balance, with plantings on one side of the main axis mirroring plantings on the other. In a formal garden, the gardener lays controlling hands on nature's exuberance. Pruning transforms shrubs into topiaries or hedges that outline geometrically shaped beds and walkways.

Informal gardens have a casual mood. Because they rely on the asymmetrical arrangement of various plant masses, informal gardens are subtler and more difficult to plan. When pruning plants, gardeners enhance their natural forms rather than carving brand-new shapes as they might in a formal setting. Informality lends itself to curving paths and borders that flow with the terrain.

Some homeowners like to combine formal and informal elements in their landscape. Symmetry and geometry, keynotes of formal gardens, work well near the house, which

Planting in rows is useful in cutting gardens, where easy access to flowers and long-stemmed plants is an important consideration. Zinnias are ideal for cutting. The more you cut them, the more new flowers come to take their place.

Spring bulbs and English daisies flourish in this entry garden. Daffodils, tulips, violet-blue grape hyacinths, and fragrant pink and purple hyacinths are planted in masses for maximum impact.

itself is a series of geometrical forms. Farther away from the house, free-flowing lines and looser edges work well. In addition, you can combine formal and informal elements by letting plants with loose, arching forms grow unrestricted within the confines of formal garden beds.

COMPOSITION

The appearance of most flower gardens changes season by season and year by year. Some changes are haphazard, due to weather, disease, prolific plants, or gifts from friends, but other changes are by design. Understanding the elements of composition empowers you to create a garden that's visually pleasing all year long.

When you look at a garden, your mind perceives it as a series of shapes and patterns. An agreeable garden plan has these shapes and patterns arranged with careful attention to the basic design principles of unity, repetition, diversity, balance, and flow. Some repetition of forms and colors is useful to unify space, but too much can be dull unless you also consider the principle of diversity. If, for example, dark red is a unifying theme in your flower garden, you can avoid monotony by introducing spots of contrasting color, by changing plant sizes and textures, and by using diverse flower forms, from bushy red sunflowers and dahlias to snapdragons, zinnias, and daylilies.

Balance refers to the visual weight of different plant combinations in the garden. If a design on one side of a central axis reflects the other side, the balance is

In late summer and early fall, this outdoor dining area displays the rich colors of 'Autumn Joy' sedum, catmint, and Frikart's aster. Ornamental grasses provide a richly textured backdrop that will persist through winter.

symmetrical. If both sides look different but carry similar visual weight, the balance is asymmetrical. Looking at a balanced design in both individual sections of the garden and the overall property gratifies the mind. Smooth transitions from one area to the next guarantee the flow of the entire design.

A focal point unifies and organizes the field of vision. A bench at the end of a flower-lined path can focus or complete a design. You can create a dramatic focal point by manipulating the scale of your garden plants. Cannas growing in a garden of medium-textured plants make an eye-catching display. For overall unity, plant scale should be consistent with the kind of garden you're creating. Rock gardens, for example, have low-growing plants that enhance rather than mask the beauty of the stones.

RIGHT PLANT IN THE RIGHT PLACE

Location, location, location—if you follow this mantra of experienced gardeners, you'll find growing flowers is easy, because the easiest flowers to grow always suit their site. Different plants need different conditions. Some species are native to the prairies of the Midwest, others to the Mediterranean region; still others belong to the forests of New England or the mountains of the Caucasus.

Yet nativity alone doesn't determine suitability; many exotic plants thrive far from their native lands. Several factors decide a plant's fitness for a location. Choosing plants that suit your climate and microclimates, including temperature, moisture, soil, light, landforms, and prevailing winds, means success.

Climate describes seasonal weather conditions in your region of the country. Heat and humidity dominate the long growing season in the Deep South, whereas extremes of hot and cold limit plant growth in the Midwest. West of the Cascades in the Pacific Northwest, a temperate climate with plentiful rainfall brings lavish English-style gardens into bloom, and in the forested lands of the Northeast, woodland species thrive in the acid soil. Coastal California's climate recalls the Mediterranean region, with its dry summers and wet winters, its windy, salt-laden air, and rocky, alkaline soil. The desert Southwest has high heat, low humidity, and particularly alkaline soil.

Microclimates, on the other hand, occur in your backyard. In cold climate regions, a flower bed on the south side of a property, against the house and with no overhanging trees, ensures the longest possible growing season. In this case, both the sunlight and its reflected heat off the wall of the house warm up the soil early in spring and keep it warm into fall.

Temperature affects a plant's survival. Before selecting plants for your garden, turn to page 92 and consult the United States Department of Agriculture's map of plant hardiness zones, relating to average annual minimum temperatures throughout the country. Find your zone and use it as a guideline when buying trees, shrubs, perennials, biennials, and bulbs.

Like temperature, rainfall varies across the country. If you live in a dry climate, don't plant moisture-loving plants unless you can provide ample irrigation, an often costly and time-consuming alternative. Conversely, if you live in a low-lying area with ample precipitation, root rot may kill some heat-loving, drought-tolerant plants.

Landforms and structures can alter growing conditions. In a backyard microclimate, a frost pocket may develop where the land dips and heavier cold air settles. Likewise, a house or a wall can block sunlight, and foundation beds

Candelabra primrose, maidenhair fern, and blue bellflower fill a nook in a moist woodland garden.

The Douglas iris and California poppies in this California meadow garden need well-drained soil in full sun.

on the north side of a house are usually best suited to shade-tolerant plants. The same wall facing south provides a warm microclimate.

The quality of light and shade can be just as important as the amount. Some plants that thrive in cool, gentle morning sunlight can wilt in the hot, slanting rays of a summer afternoon. The dense shade under a Norway maple or a building's overhang is usually dry shade and calls for plants that tolerate little water and sunlight. Because few plants can live in dry shade, the best way to deal with these situations is to grow plants away from building overhangs.

SOIL

The three main types of soil are clay, sand, and loam. Clay soil is heavy, sticky, and holds water. Composed largely of tiny, smooth-sided mineral particles that adhere closely together, it drains poorly and lacks the air pockets necessary for most plants to survive. When squeezed in the hand, wet clay soil sticks together.

On the other hand, sandy soil has relatively large, irregularly-shaped soil particles with lots of air spaces between them. It drains quickly—too quickly for the absorption of nutrients, which wash away. When squeezed, a handful of moist, sandy soil does not hold together well, but quickly crumbles and breaks apart.

Loam, made up of roughly equal parts of clay, sand, and silt (medium-sized soil particles), is ideal for growing most plants and crops because the balance of soil particle sizes achieves the best of both worlds: good water and nutrient retention with adequate air spaces and drainage. When a handful of moist loam is squeezed, it holds together but breaks apart easily when prodded with a finger.

The addition of compost or other organic matter improves the texture of nearly all types of garden soil. In clay soils it separates sticky clay particles and improves drainage. In sandy soils it retains water and nutrients. Even in optimum garden loam, organic matter can make water and nutrient retention as well as drainage even better. However, organic matter is a temporary fix for soil problems. Especially under moist conditions, it breaks down quickly and needs replenishing as often as once a year.

Soil pH, which also affects plant growth, measures acidity and alkalinity on a scale from 0 to 14. Neutral soil has a pH of 7.0; most plants grow well in a slightly acid soil between pH 5.5 and 6.5. In the plains and open country of western North America, soils tend to be alkaline with a pH above 7.0; in the moist, forested regions of eastern North America, acid soils typically prevail. You can test your soil to determine its pH level, or observe the plants that grow nearby. Rhododendrons and azaleas thrive in acid soil, whereas cinquefoil, rock rose, and pinks are examples of plants that perform well in alkaline soil. Knowing your soil type and pH helps you find plants that do well in the specific conditions of your yard.

Rock gardens don't have to be high in the mountains. This sunny pond surrounded by stone is planted with water lilies and rimmed with sea lavender and 'May Night' salvia.

Bougainvillea freely climbs the outer wall of this contemporary home in the Southwest; a mesquite tree grows nearby. A raised bed, where soil quality is easily controlled, contains more flowering plants.

16 EASY FLOWER GARDENS

Blue rosemary, ground morning glory, verbena, and germander sage cascade down a dry slope amid splashes of sea lavender and agapanthus. See page 25 for more about this garden.

This chapter addresses 16 commonly encountered landscape challenges and provides solutions. Each design illustrates principles described in previous chapters and shows how to use plants from the "Gallery of Easy Flowers" (pages 46–91). From foundation plantings to solutions for dry slopes and soggy patches, you'll see how flower gardens can integrate your home with its surroundings. You'll discover suggestions for formal and informal plantings that are ideal for urban curbsides; under trees and around lampposts in the lawn; gardens seen mostly at dusk; and gardens to attract birds and butterflies. Incorporate these plans as is into your landscape, or use them to stimulate ideas as you design your own garden.

FLOWERS AT THE FOUNDATION

The joy of a foundation planting is that you see it close up and often. It's the perfect place for flowers, where their form, scent, and color can be intimately experienced. If you're a traditionalist, flowers can supplement your evergreen foundation shrubs instead of replacing them.

Foundation plants can emphasize architectural elements, such as your primary entrance. Consider placing tall plants on either side of the front door to punctuate its verticality. Create a visual transition from the architecture of the house to the irregular natural landscape by installing mounded, rounded plants at the corners of the house.

Flowering broad-leaved evergreens add stability and pleasing color to tall foundations. Green is especially important in northern climates, where snow covers the ground for months on end and spring comes late most years. Deciduous flowering shrubs, on the other hand, give foundations seasonal variety, including flowers, summer foliage, fall color, and an interesting winter branching pattern.

Because foundations are not as high as they were a century ago, you do not have to use large plants. Annual and perennial flowers can often fill the foundation area with a desirable splash of color that draws the attention away from low bands of concrete.

Flowers at the foundation can soften the harsh lines of the front path. Massed annuals of one color attract your gaze to the flowers and away from defects of house or property.

Hanging baskets and window boxes are other accessories that decorate porches and front walks during the growing season. By selecting flowers for these containers that harmonize with your home and the plantings around it, you can unify and enhance the perception of your house from the road.

SHADY FOUNDATION

This north-facing foundation planting bears soft pink, pale yellow, and lacy white flowers all year. Colorful foliage provides additional interest, from the soft-textured blue tones of fringed bleeding heart, meadow rue, yellow corydalis, and columbine to the dark purple-green of coral bells. Climbing hydrangeas turn gold in fall; the rhododendrons and Lenten rose stay green all winter.

PLANT LIST
1. 'Album' catawba rhododendron, p. 82
2. 'Ruby Spice' summersweet, p. 58
3. Lavender mist meadow rue, p. 86
4. Climbing hydrangea, p. 68
5. Yellow corydalis, p. 59
6. 'Finale' Chinese astilbe, p. 53
7. Yellow columbine, p. 52
8. 'Luxuriant' bleeding heart, p. 61
9. 'Palace Purple' coral bells, p. 67
10. Lenten rose, p. 66
11. Pink azalea, p. 82, in pot as standard
12. 'Victorian Rose White' impatiens, p. 68, in window boxes
13. False climbing hydrangea, p. 68

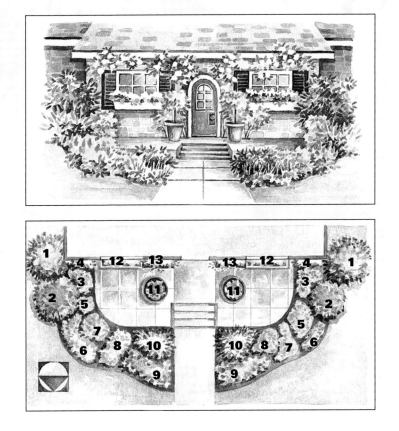

SUNNY FOUNDATION

Throughout the growing season, this low foundation planting glows with flowers of white, lemon yellow, pink, and blue. Inside the entrance court, the composition is more formal and symmetrical. Outside, the design assumes a looser, more informal look.

PLANT LIST
1. 'Orbit Pink' geranium, p. 79
2. 'Snowcloth' sweet alyssum, p. 72
3. 'Havana Appleblossom' tobacco, p. 76
4. Jackman clematis, p. 57
5. 'Butterfly Blue' pincushion flower, p. 84
6. 'Polarsommer' mullein, p. 88
7. 'Max Frei' soapwort, p. 84
8. 'Happy Returns' daylily, p. 67
9. 'Miss Manners' obedient plant, p. 81
10. 'Moonbeam' coreopsis, p. 59
11. 'Blue Danube' Stokes' aster, p. 85
12. 'Fuji White' balloon flower, p. 81
13. 'Watermelon' Oriental poppy, p. 78, interplanted with Russian sage, p. 79
14. 'Marshall's Delight' bee balm, p. 74
15. 'Six Hills Giant' catmint, p. 76
16. 'Sarah Bernhardt' peony, p. 78

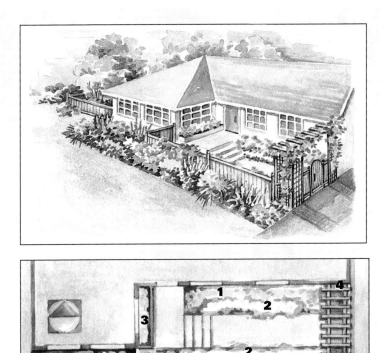

Greeting the Street

Old-fashioned cottage gardens are small. They contain a jumble of useful perennials and self-sowing annuals packed on either side of a central path. Here we bring the ancient cottage tradition up to date. Our path is a city sidewalk. This sunny cottage garden exists not to provide food, medicine, and stewing herbs for the family but to enhance the curb appeal of an urban house with a small front yard. When the plants mature, this informal design will provide drifts of harmonious colors that spill over the curb and soften the hard, straight edges of the sidewalk. The result is a welcoming garden that adds to the charm of the house while presenting a neighborly gift to passersby.

Although the plants in this garden are, for the most part, neither edible nor useful, they fulfill several requirements for their prominent location, where the air contains exhaust fumes and the soil is poor. To grow this garden, first dig compost or aged manure into the soil to improve drainage, moisture retention, and nutrient balance. The perennials are tough and enduring, and the annual snapdragons and larkspurs self-sow. Moreover, these flowers have prolonged blooming seasons. If they are started indoors, snapdragons can bloom from spring to fall. Especially in cool-summer climates, successive sowings of larkspur will provide color all summer. With little effort, catmint, coreopsis, lavender, purple coneflower, and 'The Fairy' rose keep their good looks for weeks on end.

For earlier flowering, broadcast corms of 'Barr's Purple' crocus before adding a final inch of topsoil to the bed. This self-sowing, squirrel-resistant crocus blooms for several weeks in early spring. It's an excellent harbinger of both warmer weather and the bed's cool colors to come.

Plant List

1. 'Summer Sun' false sunflower, p. 66
2. 'Giant Imperial' larkspur, p. 58
3. 'Magnus' purple coneflower, p. 62
4. 'Moonshine' yarrow, p. 50
5. 'Munstead' English lavender, p. 70
6. 'The Fairy' polyantha rose, p. 82
7. 'Becky' Shasta daisy, p. 57
8. 'Blue Hill' salvia, p. 83
9. 'Indian Spring' hollyhock, p. 51
10. 'Blue Wonder' catmint, p. 76
11. 'Heavenly Blue' morning glory, p. 69
12. 'Bath's Pink' dianthus, p. 61
13. 'Lipstick Silver' snapdragon, p. 52
14. 'Purple Dome' aster, p. 53
15. 'Moonbeam' coreopsis, p. 59

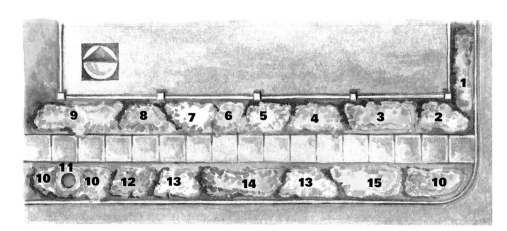

GARDEN GATEWAY

As in love so in gardens, opposites attract. In this bright garden of annual flowers, the balance of opposite hues leans toward hot, with pink, orange, magenta, and lots of unifying yellow. Soothing greens and whites blend the electric colors into a cohesive whole.

Draped in the airy, fine-textured foliage of cypress vine, the arched gateway at one end of the garden frames the view, leading your gaze down a brick path to the garden's focal point, an urn of 'Aurora' New Zealand flax, with red-, pink-, and yellow-striped leaves, echoed on either side by the dramatic yellow-striped leaves of 'Bengal Tiger' canna.

Seen from the drive, the annuals outside the picket fence indicate the varied vibrant colors inside the gate. 'Century Yellow' cockscomb and the dark-eyed golden blooms of 6-inch-high creeping zinnia and black-eyed Susan vine frame the neon purple globe amaranth. In front, 'Purple Wave' petunia carpets the ground in brilliant magenta.

Inside the fence the contrast of clear blue flossflower with orange cosmos and Mexican sunflower heightens the drama. Likewise the golden gloriosa daisy and magenta wheat celosia are near complements that add visual energy. Other flowers perceived as complementary include pink vinca and the pale chartreuse 'Envy' zinnia.

PLANT LIST

1. 'Purple Wave' petunia, p. 80
2. 'Mandarin Yellow' creeping zinnia, p. 84
3. 'Buddy' globe amaranth, p. 64
4. 'Century Yellow' cockscomb, p. 56
5. 'Suzie' black-eyed Susan vine, p. 87
6. Cypress vine, p. 69
7. 'Pink Candle' wheat celosia, p. 56
8. 'Domino White' flowering tobacco, p. 76
9. 'Blue Lagoon' flossflower, p. 51
10. 'Indian Summer' gloriosa daisy, p. 83
11. 'White Rocket' snapdragon, p. 52
12. 'Pretty in Rose' vinca, p. 56
13. 'Envy' zinnia, p. 90
14. 'Diablo' cosmos, p. 60
15. 'Blue Tango' flossflower, p. 51
16. 'Goldilocks' gloriosa daisy, p. 83
17. 'Goldfinger' Mexican sunflower, p. 87
18. 'Bengal Tiger' canna, p. 55
19. 'Blush Cooler' vinca, p. 56
20. 'Aurora' New Zealand flax
21. 'Bradford' Callery pear tree
22. 'Longwood' wintergreen euonymus

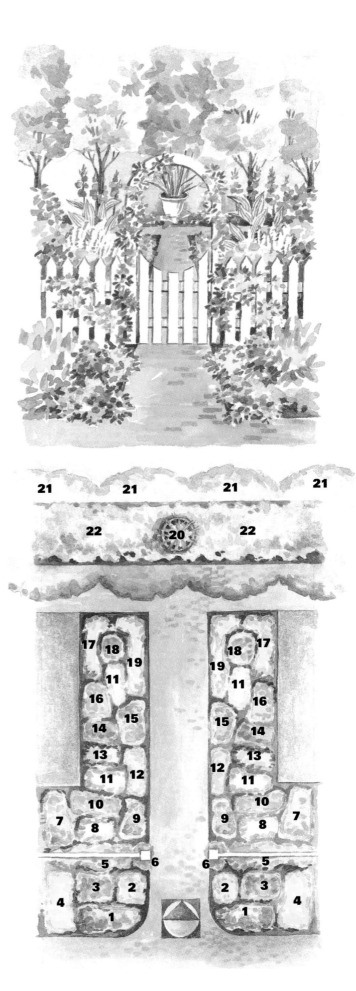

FENCE-LINE FORMAL BORDER

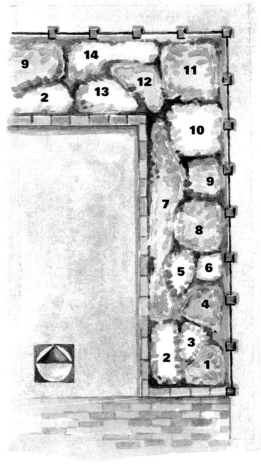

This traditional mixed border contains herbaceous perennials, bulbs, and long-flowering shrubs that peak in late spring and early summer when the iris, peony, foxglove, rose, Shasta daisy, and pincushion flower are all in bloom.

Careful layering from back to front gives this border a lavish, undulating architecture. Against a wrought-iron fence, taller plants form the back layer, including a 10-foot chaste tree in one corner and spiky foxgloves, which grow up to 5 feet high. The rose, garden phlox, lily, aster, and Shasta daisy provide 3- to 4-foot stature also useful in the rear. Lavender, iris, and herbaceous peony add midrange height, and pincushion flower and coral bells carpet the foreground.

Cool colors predominate, giving the garden a tranquil effect. All season, a ribbon of lavender to violet runs through the border with pincushion flower, Frikart's aster, 'Heavenly Blue' Siberian iris, 'Hidcote Blue' English lavender, and chaste tree. 'Frederic Mistral' rose and 'Raspberry Sundae' peony provide elegant tints of pink. An abundance of white flowers brings lightness and shimmer.

Brick edging at the front and sides of the border adds to the garden's formality. The flat bricks provide a touch of warm color and, more importantly, make it easy to mow the grass without trimming the edges by hand.

PLANT LIST

1. 'Hidcote Blue' English lavender, p. 70
2. 'Snowcap' Shasta daisy, p. 57
3. 'Mont Blanc' Asiatic lily, p. 71
4. 'Frederic Mistral' Romantica rose, p. 82
5. 'White Swirl' Siberian iris, p. 69
6. 'David' garden phlox, p. 80
7. 'Butterfly Blue' pincushion flower, p. 84
8. 'Raspberry Sundae' peony, p. 78
9. 'Heavenly Blue' Siberian iris, p. 69
10. 'Becky' Shasta daisy, p. 57
11. Chaste tree, p. 90
12. 'Monch' Frickart's aster, p. 53
13. 'Pewter Veil' coral bells, p. 67
14. 'Alba' foxglove, p. 61

Although this garden requires some maintenance for maximum bloom, the upkeep is simple. Stake peonies with peony rings in early spring when the foliage begins to emerge. Deadhead foxgloves to improve their appearance after flowering, but let one or two plants go to seed so new plants will form. Deadhead the rose, Shasta daisies, and pincushion flower to prolong their bloom. Prune the rose back each fall to encourage abundant blooms the next summer.

FLOWERY HEDGE

Your next-door neighbors may be your best friends, but sometimes you want to be alone. You don't need a solid barrier between your land and theirs. You'd just like to create a sense of solitude and at the same time beautify your property.

Seen from the house, this flowery screen looks seamless and impassable, but up close you see three clear sections—a baffle design that lends a feeling of mystery and privacy while providing a neighborly connection. Walking toward the hedge, you're lured to the paths that open up to your neighbors' land.

Height, multiseason interest, and late-summer peak of bloom are the main reasons for choosing the classic combination of perennials in this design. In flower, the ornamental grass 'Sarabande' miscanthus grows 6 feet tall with narrow leaves. Massed, its fine-textured foliage creates elegant, billowing fountains in the landscape. In the wind, the grass rustles and sways. Coppery gold tassels emerge in August.

Yet the garden value of miscanthus lasts beyond the growing season into March, when most gardeners cut it back. When the top of the plant goes dormant in autumn, the grass, now a glowing, warm tan, remains upright. In the winter sun, ice sparkles on leaves and seed heads. Snow turns these grasses into lofty mounds that right themselves as it melts.

Arkansas amsonia also has a long season of interest. In late spring, the plant bears terminal clusters of light blue, starry flowers. During summer, its fine-textured leaves and upright stems echo the texture of 'Sarabande' miscanthus, giving amsonia the appearance of a handsome shrub for the rest of the season. In September, its feathery leaves flame into incandescent yellow. Likewise, oakleaf hydrangea, a deciduous shrub, bears dramatic conical flower heads in summer, but its red-toned fall foliage is as impressive as its blooms. The flowers slowly turn pink and persist into fall.

Golden-rayed black-eyed Susan flowers from July through September and has interesting blackish seed heads that are striking against snow. For an astonishing two to three months, its neon yellow blooms offer a striking counterpoint to the more muted pinks and golds of this composition. The blooms of succulent 'Autumn Joy' sedum start out light green in early summer, then change to rosy pink in August and by September to a deep rust that lingers most of the winter. 'Gateway' Joe-Pye weed also peaks in late summer and remains interesting well into winter with persistent seed heads. From July through September, its mauve-pink flowers flourish on bushy 5- to 6-foot stems, echoing in a larger scale the pink-to-russet tones and flower form of 'Autumn Joy' sedum.

Because their foliage emerges late in spring, just in time to hide the yellowing leaves of bulbs, the black-eyed Susan, Joe-Pye weed, and miscanthus are perfect for underplanting with bulbs for early-season effect.

PLANT LIST

1. 'Goldsturm' black-eyed Susan, p. 83
2. 'Sarabande' miscanthus, p. 74
3. Arkansas amsonia, p. 52
4. 'Gateway' Joe-Pye weed, p. 63
5. 'Snowflake' oakleaf hydrangea, p. 68
6. 'Autumn Joy' sedum, p. 85

ISLAND IN THE SUN

No matter where you live in North America, a Victorian-style lawn bed can turn your garden into a tropical paradise. Whether for whimsy, for practical purposes, or to enhance a Victorian house, an island of showy annuals and tender perennials can brighten your landscape with bold blooms and big, colorful leaves from June to frost.

The illustrated garden is an updated tropical island of red, gold, and burgundy flowers with accents in chartreuse, pink, and white. If that sounds splashy, well, it is! The design follows the lead of the house, a Victorian "painted lady" with several hues of paint and a fanciful gingerbread rail. Both house and garden embody ornamentation for its own sake. Look closely, however, and you see the flamboyant garden design also has a practical side.

This sunny island solves the problem posed by the lamppost lighting the driveway of the house. Setting a lamppost in a lawn rather than in a bed makes mowing difficult. Because most lawn mowers cannot mow close to a post, homeowners cut the surrounding grass by hand, a slow and tedious task. For gardeners with riding mowers, a curving island can eliminate sharp and potentially dangerous turns. As long as the arcs of the island are sweeping in shape, the grass is easy to mow. Use garden hose to lay out a kidney-shaped or rounded bed, or stakes and string to mark the edges of an angled one. To keep grass from escaping into the island, a brick barrier or a deep-set plastic edge can block the spread of roots. Mulching the bed reduces weeds and helps retain moisture.

Repetition of plants and colors helps integrate the tropical bed with the foundation planting. White-flowered foundation hydrangeas, a Victorian favorite, and white tuberous begonias in the foundation moderate the island's brilliance, while moss rose in the bed and the foundation unifies the entry garden's overall design. The lamppost defines the bed's architectural center, on which grows purple-flowered hyacinth bean vine. Glowing chartreuse sweet potato vine spills from baskets hung on the post. Planted near the bed's center, 'Red King Humbert' canna is a structural plant that grows up to 7 feet tall with 3-foot burgundy leaves and dark red flowers. It richly complements the burgundy sunflower, the chartreuse flowering tobacco and love-lies-bleeding, and the violet spider flower, further enhancing the garden's tropical effect.

PLANT LIST

1. 'Sundial Peppermint' moss rose, p. 81
2. 'Lavender Lady' globe amaranth, p. 64
3. 'Sparkler Wine' cockscomb, p. 56
4. 'Rustic Colors' gloriosa daisy, p. 83
5. Langsdorf's flowering tobacco, p. 76
6. 'Viridis' love-lies-bleeding, p. 51
7. 'Violet Queen' spider flower, p. 58
8. 'Red King Humbert' canna, p. 55
9. 'Velvet Queen' sunflower, p. 65
10. 'French Vanilla' marigold, p. 86
11. Hyacinth bean on post, p. 62
12. 'Marguarite' sweet potato vine in hanging baskets, p. 69
13. 'Paint Splash Pink' wax begonia, p. 54
14. 'Nonstop White' tuberous begonia, p. 54
15. 'Annabelle' smooth hydrangea, p. 68

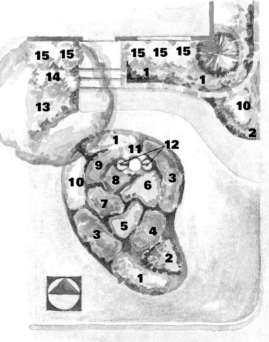

A SHADY ISLE

Trees are even more vulnerable than lampposts to lawn mower damage. If a tree is young and newly planted, a lawn mower whack can be fatal. Mature trees are also susceptible to damage. Cutting the grass next to a tree often results in gashed bark. Bark injuries create entry sites for pests and diseases. Left untreated, an injured tree can sicken and die.

The solution to this landscape dilemma is an island bed that eliminates the need for grass. Grass grows with difficulty under trees. Many ground covers, however, thrive in shade, and these spreading, healthy plants look better around tree roots than bare soil and wisps of grass.

Island beds can connect two or more trees and shrubs into an integrated design. These islands, shaded by tree foliage, unify mature plantings in your existing landscape. Instead of trying to make design sense of individual trees, shrubs, ground covers, and flowers, you can build a plan with fewer, larger elements.

An island is a chance to explore the relationships between the heights, shapes, and silhouettes of plants that can create a grander statement when taken together than when seen alone. To unite these disparate landscape elements requires adding one or more plants with a rounded form to bridge the space between trees.

In this plan, where a shady bed protects two flowering dogwoods, evergreen pink-flowering azaleas fill this connecting role,

echoing the azaleas along the foundation of the house. The rounded masses of Lenten rose—also evergreen, with flowers over two months in late winter and earliest spring—provide a similar complementary effect.

A ground cover of perennials distinguishes the borders of the island from the surrounding grass. The soft mounds of 'Snowdrift' fringed bleeding heart reach a peak of white bloom at azalea time that keeps repeating for an astonishing summer-long season. 'Luxuriant' bleeding heart provides a similar effect in pink. The silver-leaved spotted dead nettle and reddish-bronze-leaved coral bells add interesting foliage color and low ground-covering form all season long.

Easy ground covers and perennials require far less upkeep than lawn. There may be mulch to spread, an occasional weed to pull, and an annual cleaning, but that's not much compared with the weekly care a large lawn can require. Remember that mulch should be no deeper than 3 inches. Also, keep it out of the crowns of perennials and away from the base of trees, where it can cause rot.

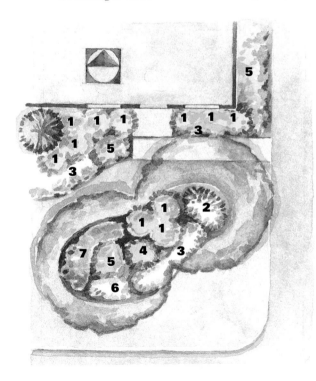

PLANT LIST

1. Pink azalea, p. 82
2. Lenten rose, p. 66
3. 'Snowdrift' fringed bleeding heart, p. 61
4. Bear's foot hellebore, p. 66
5. 'Luxuriant' fringed bleeding heart, p. 61
6. 'Beacon Silver' spotted dead nettle, p. 69
7. 'Bressingham Bronze' coral bells, p. 67

A DAMP CORNER

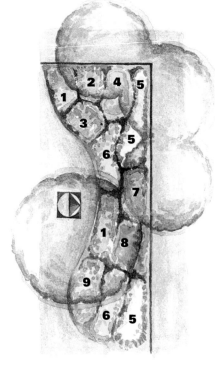

PLANT LIST

1. 'Petite Delight' bee balm,
   p. 74
2. Yellow flag iris,
   p. 69
3. 'Concord Grape' spiderwort, p. 87
4. Swamp milkweed,
   p. 53
5. 'Blue River' hibiscus, p. 67
6. 'Yellow Futurity' canna,
   p. 55
7. 'Gateway' Joe-Pye weed,
   p. 63
8. 'Vivid' obedient plant, p. 81
9. 'Rheinland' astilbe,
   p. 53

B ringing color to a wet spot on your property is harder than you'd think. Many plants drown when their roots are submerged in water. Wet soil can produce root rot, and plants with rotten roots lack vigor and eventually die. Symptoms include yellow leaves at the base of the plant, followed by yellowing at the top.

Damp spots have different causes. Clay soils, composed of tiny mineral particles that attract water molecules and stick together when wet, are often poorly drained. When waterlogged, clay soil lacks adequate aeration, which means oxygen can't reach the roots of a growing plant and carbon dioxide can't escape from the earth into the atmosphere.

The topography of the land sometimes creates wet soil. Water collects in low areas after a rain. Seasonal streams may appear in spring when snow melts and rain is abundant. In some neighborhoods, developers shape the land so rain and runoff flow into swales—dips in the contour of the land—which channel the water into ponds, lakes, or bays. Water may also collect in neighborhood drainage culverts specified by town planners.

A swale or seasonal stream flows through the rear edge of this garden. Partly shaded by three deciduous trees on the neighbor's property and one in the homeowner's lawn, the garden features plants that thrive in damp soil. The cheery color scheme balances plants in bright purple, yellow, and pink. Located at the back of the yard along the fence, this informal garden creates a delightful, long-blooming focal point from a deck or family room.

The plants in this design are well equipped for wet soils. They will let you create the look you want without extensive work to raise the soil level for improved drainage. 'Petite Delight' bee balm blooms from early to late summer in deep, intense rose, a color repeated by the summer-blooming 'Rheinland' astilbe and the late summer blooms of obedient plant. Although yellow flag iris flowers in early summer, its sword-shaped leaves, which grow up to 5 feet tall, persist long after flowering ends. The narrow leaves of 'Concord Grape' spiderwort are a pleasing counterpoint to the iris foliage, and the intense purple flowers are the perfect opposite of the bright yellow iris flowers and the flowers of the dwarf 'Yellow Futurity' canna. The milkweed and Joe-Pye weed lend a tall, soft touch with mauve-pink flowers later in the summer, and the 'Blue River' hibiscus (named after the river where it was found) provides white, dinner-plate-sized flowers all summer on tall, bushy plants.

A DRY SLOPE

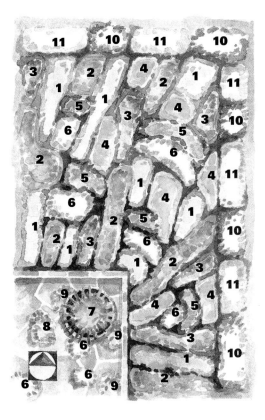

Landscaping a dry, sunny slope poses problems. The first problem is erosion, the gradual wearing away of the soil on the hillside by wind, rain, and the downward tug of gravity. Another problem is the soil itself, which in this case is dry and rocky with low fertility. A third problem is runoff. When it rains, moisture can't penetrate the already parched earth. Water hits the ground, skims its surface, and runs down the slope.

This California coastal garden faces some added challenges: salt-laden sea breezes, intense sunshine, and the alternating dry summers and wet winters of a Mediterranean climate. The plan takes its cue from the seashore location. Blue-gray foliage and blossoms ranging from steel blue and lavender to intense cobalt and violet course down the slope like ocean waves. The floods of low-growing rosemary, ground morning glory, verbena and germander sage lap and overlap and occasionally break against boulders in blue sprays of sea lavender that drip with the white foam of sweet alyssum.

Tall blue sprays of agapanthus in a large pot carry the theme at the base of the retaining wall. Lavender 'Moerheimeri' Mexican daisy and sweet alyssum are planted in the cracks of the flagstone-in-sand patio and allowed to reseed in casual splashes, as are the sky-blue flowers of 'Blue Sapphire' perennial flax. At the top of the slope, shrubby New Zealand tea-tree and sageleaf rock rose form a windbreak as well as a backdrop of white flowers in winter and spring.

Some plants are adapted to the difficult conditions of a dry, sunny slope. Rosemary, sage, and creeping verbena, for example, contain volatile oils that protect them from drying out. Ground morning glory has silvery, hairy foliage that reflects heat and protects from desiccation. Sea lavender, rock rose, and New Zealand tea-tree have waxy or leathery leaves that help prevent water loss. Many plants native to the Mediterranean, South Africa, and Australia are well-adapted to the moist, mild winters and warm, dry summers of California.

The plants chosen for this plan are mostly low and prostrate, spreading by runners or rooting branches to form a dense network of roots excellent for holding soil. Ground covers also protect the soil by shading the ground beneath the leaves. Less moisture evaporates, and the network of roots helps absorb every drop of water that reaches the earth. And the trailing forms are beautiful as they hug the ground and drape over the wall.

PLANT LIST

1. 'Lockwood de Forest' rosemary
2. Ground morning glory, p. 59
3. 'Tapien Blue' verbena, p. 89
4. Germander sage, p. 83
5. Sea lavender, p. 71
6. 'Snowcloth' sweet alyssum, p. 72
7. 'Bressingham Blue' agapanthus, p. 50
8. 'Moerheimeri' Mexican daisy (fleabane), p. 62
9. 'Blue Sapphire' perennial flax, p. 72
10. 'Snow White' New Zealand tea-tree, p. 71
11. Sageleaf rock rose, p. 57

Bower of Flowers

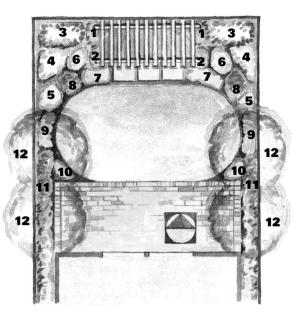

This garden is dreamy and romantic for much of the growing season, thanks to a combination of soft, harmonious pinks and whites and airy clouds of flowers. The focal point, a trellised bower, lies opposite the brick patio of the townhouse, creating an axis through the center of the property. The brick patio, the garden, and its bower become an extension of the architecture—an outdoor room where the owners can read, relax, dine, and entertain.

Although symmetry is usually associated with formality, this garden is far from stiff. In fact, it demonstrates an effective combination of formal and informal elements. The plan is symmetrical, but the plants themselves possess a loose, casual character far removed from the meticulous topiaries and geometrical shapes associated with the formal style.

Reliable pale pink 'New Dawn' rose clambers up a trellis, paired with 'Frances Rivis' alpine clematis. The clematis bears droopy, pale blue, cap-shaped blossoms of exceptional grace. After the spring flowers fade, puffy silver seed heads replace them, adding another season of interest to the plant and complementing the rose.

Like the clematis that weaves through the rose canes, most of the other plants in this garden are weavers. Boltonia is tall and clump-forming with little daisy flowers. It will lean gracefully into the plants around it. White gaura has long stems tipped with little flowers that bend and weave through nearby plants and blend with other fine-textured flowers: 'Hewitt's Double' meadow rue, which produces airy sprays of tiny pink fluffs; and

PLANT LIST

1. 'New Dawn' climbing rose, p. 82
2. 'Frances Rivis' alpine clematis, p. 57
3. 'Snowbank' boltonia, p. 54
4. White gaura, p. 64
5. 'Hewitt's Double' meadow rue, p. 86
6. 'Persian Jewels' love-in-a-mist, p. 77
7. 'Nora Barlow' columbine, p. 52
8. 'Mont Rose' tree mallow, p. 70
9. 'Pewter Moon' coral bells, p. 67
10. 'Bridget Bloom' heucherella, p. 67
11. Japanese bleeding heart, p. 61, followed by 'Mosaic Violet' impatiens, p. 68
12. 'Royal Purple' smokebush, p. 60

annual love-in-a-mist, with delicate blue, white, and pink flowers, threadlike leaves, and puffy seed heads. Staggered sowings will provide constant love-in-a-mist bloom.

Between the pink frills of 'Nora Barlow' columbine and the silver-toned burgundy leaves of 'Pewter Moon' coral bells lies an icy pink mound of 'Mont Rose' tree mallow. Under clouds of deep pink smokebush plumes is a large stand of old-fashioned Japanese bleeding heart, hard to beat for romance. This bleeding heart dies back soon after bloom in late spring, when the impatiens underneath assumes a starring role. In front, heucherella's multiple pink flower wands rise above an attractive clump of leaves and last for months.

Woodland Walk

Shady gardens possess a special beauty. The best ones rely on the colors and textures of leaves for maximum effect. With planning, a low-light garden may contain leaves that run the gamut of greens to gold, purple, blue, and silver, with some leaves lined or splashed with two or more hues. Specifically, silver, blue, and golden leaves, along with foliage variegated with white, cream, or yellow, stand out in low light. Blooming flowers add another decorative dimension. Shade-loving flowers tend toward pastels—pink, blue, and lavender—and white, all of which bring a delicate beauty to the shade.

The woodland walk shown here derives its open shade from three thornless honeylocust trees. This garden is meant for viewing up close, with a walk that winds through densely planted beds. In early spring, before the trees leaf out, the beds are already blooming with the light green and dark purple flowers of Lenten rose. The exotic-looking blossoms are hardy enough to bloom through snow, and they remain effective for two months or more.

Later in spring the fringed bleeding heart begins its spring-to-fall show, followed by the colorful sprays of coral bells and heucherella. The coral bells not only bear long-lasting, airy flower wands, they also turn into handsome clumps of attractive foliage ranging from the plum silver leaves of 'Velvet Night' to the dark purple leaves of 'Palace Purple'. In midsummer the spikes of white and deep rose foxglove are echoed in the white and pink plumes of the astilbes and the airy clouds of lavender mist meadow rue. The pink-and-

yellow flowers of 'Serotina' honeysuckle perfume the air until frost. At the season's finale, the dwarf 'Hummingbird' summersweet adds honey-sweet fragrance from white spikes of flowers, and concludes the show with brilliant yellow fall leaves.

PLANT LIST

1. 'White Gloria' astilbe, p. 53
2. 'Palace Purple' coral bells, p. 67
3. Woodland tobacco, p. 76
4. Royal Heritage Hybrids Lenten rose, p. 66
5. 'Raspberry Regal' coral bells, p. 67
6. 'Foxy' foxglove, p. 61
7. 'Dayglow Pink' heucherella, p. 67
8. 'Hummingbird' summersweet, p. 58
9. 'Serotina' honeysuckle, p. 72
10. Bear's foot hellebore, p. 66
11. Lavender mist meadow rue, p. 86
12. 'Bressingham Beauty' astilbe, p. 53
13. 'Alba' foxglove, p. 61
14. 'Erica' astilbe, p. 53
15. 'Snowflakes' fringed bleeding heart, p. 61
16. 'Velvet Night' coral bells, p. 67
17. Thornless honeylocust

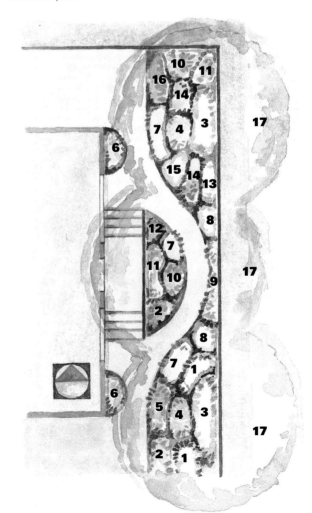

FORMAL PARTERRE

Parterres are low, patterned plantings that look best from above, where their formal shapes can be clearly seen. This pink, white, and gold townhouse garden, based on a parterre that can be strolled around or seen from a balcony, gives big presence to a small space. Its symmetrical layout has a central axis leading to a focal point, a large fountain at the rear. Anchoring the center of the garden is an urn with a pink miniature rose.

Effective layering of plants makes good use of limited space. Pink and white butterfly bushes underplanted with golden 'Stella de Oro' daylilies line the long sides of the garden. This remarkable daylily peaks in early summer, then continues blooming nearly all summer. Its emerging leaves neatly hide the foliage of the spring daffodils underneath. At the rear of the garden are 'Forest Pansy' eastern redbud trees, with deep pink flowers at daffodil time and burgundy foliage all summer. Under them are drifts of summer-long pink and white fringed bleeding hearts.

Short boxwood hedges define the borders of the parterre. Inside the color fields are layered plantings of pink 'Angelique' tulips and 'Thai Silk Appleblossom' California poppies; the poppies are directly sown in late winter before the bulbs begin to emerge. They bloom as the tulips finish and continue to late summer, when they are replaced with the smoky pinks of 'Antique Shades' pansy. In late spring, as its white tulips are finishing, the central color field is planted with spiky 'White Rocket' snapdragons. Arising from the snapdragons in late summer on tall, bare stems, the pink, lilylike flowers of "naked ladies" (hardy amaryllis) perform a brief but spectacular show.

PLANT LIST

1. 'Angelique' tulip, p. 88, overseeded with 'Thai Silk Appleblossom' California poppy, p. 63, followed by 'Antique Shades' pansy, p. 89
2. 'Minnow' daffodil, p. 75, and 'Mount Tacoma' tulip, p. 88, followed by 'White Rocket' snapdragon, p. 52, and hardy amaryllis, p. 73
3. 'Mary Marshall' miniature rose, p. 82
4. 'Pink Delight' butterfly bush, p. 54
5. 'White Profusion' butterfly bush, p. 54
6. 'Thalia' and 'Barrett Browning' daffodils, p. 75, followed by 'Stella de Oro' daylily, p. 67
7. 'Forest Pansy' eastern redbud underplanted with 'Luxuriant' and 'Snowdrift' fringed bleeding hearts, p. 61
8. Boxwood hedge

FLOWERS FOR WILDLIFE

Songbirds, hummingbirds, and butterflies bring a garden to life and give it a larger purpose. A successful wildlife garden provides songbirds with diverse plants for cover and food. In this garden, serviceberry and chokeberry produce early-season berries; blueberry and elder nourish birds in midsummer; dogwood, hawthorn, and crabapple fruit in fall; and winterberry offers berries in winter. A pool near the deck offers water for drinking and bathing, and sunflowers, Joseph's coat, coneflower, and aster produce seeds. The garden also contains bird feeders for bringing birds up close, and a hidden brush pile for shelter and nesting.

Honeysuckle growing on the deck rail attracts hummingbirds. Other vines and shrubs attractive to hummingbirds include weigela, scarlet runner bean, cardinal climber, cypress vine, and butterfly bush. Hummingbirds are drawn to flowers with a tubular shape that accommodate their long bills. They prefer red flowers set horizontally on a stem or dangling away from foliage, so they can hover while nectaring. Some flowers they enjoy include coral bells, sage, Mexican sunflower, and bee balm. Other annuals attractive to hummingbirds grow in pots on the deck near nectar feeders: lantana, geranium, petunia, zinnia, and mandevilla.

Butterflies also thrive in this garden; it contains larval host plants for caterpillars, such as spicebush, aster, and milkweed, as well as nectar plants for adults, water, and shelter from the wind. Butterfly bush, Joe-Pye weed, butterfly weed, swamp milkweed, aster, astilbe, sunflowers, lavender, oregano, sedum, sage, and purple coneflower are butterfly magnets.

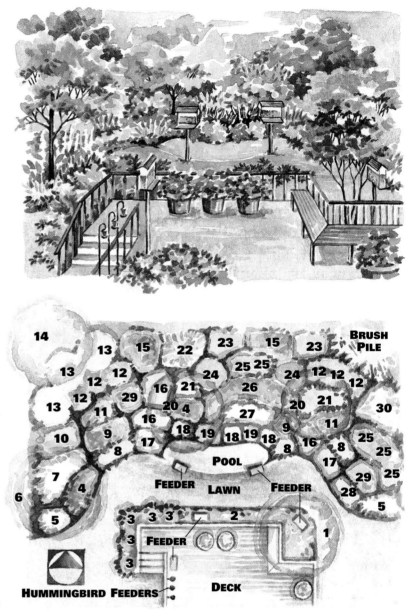

PLANT LIST

1. 'Wonderberry' flowering dogwood
2. Trumpet honeysuckle, p. 72, along deck rail
3. 'Bristol Ruby' weigela
4. 'Mt. St. Helens' coral bells, p. 67
5. 'Alba' English lavender, p. 70
6. 'Donald Wyman' crabapple
7. Woodland tobacco, p. 76
8. 'Brilliant' sedum, p. 85
9. 'Coral Nymph' Texas sage, p. 83
10. 'Fanny's Aster' New England aster, p. 53
11. 'Marshall's Delight' bee balm, p. 74
12. Highbush blueberry
13. 'Aurea' American elder
14. 'Forest Prince' serviceberry
15. 'Torch' Mexican sunflower, p. 87
16. 'Magnus' purple coneflower, p. 62
17. 'May Night' salvia, p. 83
18. 'Winter Red' winterberry with one 'Southern Gentleman' winterberry for pollination
19. 'Brilliantissima' chokeberry
20. 'Winter King' hawthorn
21. 'Superba' Chinese astilbe, p. 53
22. Joseph's coat, p. 51
23. 'Mammoth Russian' sunflower, p. 65
24. Spicebush
25. 'Pink Delight' butterfly bush, p. 54
26. 'Gateway' Joe-Pye weed, p. 63
27. Summersweet, p. 58
28. 'Herrenhausen' oregano, p. 78
29. Butterfly weed, p. 53
30. Swamp milkweed, p. 53

PICTURE-PERFECT PATIO

This patio, perfect for relaxation or entertaining friends, makes an appealing outdoor room. It has flagstone paving for a floor, stone retaining walls to suggest enclosure, and an arc of Kousa dogwoods as a backdrop. Water in a rectangular pool, the patio's focal point, is a calming presence. Although the plantings are symmetrically arranged, they are loose and informal. Plants grow in pockets among the flagstones, in raised beds, or draped over rock walls, and they change by the season.

Soothing blue flowers are a constant theme from early spring through fall. Most of the perennials are underplanted with spring-blooming blue varieties of hyacinth, grape hyacinth, and scilla. 'Blue Spades' columbine, 'Butterfly Blue' pincushion flower, and a blue Japanese iris in the pool and in the bed above follow spring's end; the pincushion flower blooms for a seemingly endless season all summer and well into fall. 'Blue Danube' Stokes' aster adds its notes from early to late summer, when the late-blooming but spectacular blue plumbago takes over. Used generously in drifts and planting pockets, the plumbago peaks in late summer with the electric blue hydrangeas, which wrap around the garden in a powerful circle of blue.

Bursts of intense pink, magenta, chartreuse, and moonlight yellow add verve to what would otherwise be a too-peaceful blue composition. On the arbor, the pink-and-cream flowers of 'Serotina' honeysuckle perfume the air all summer. Bear's foot hellebore adds chartreuse flowers in early spring, the flowering tobacco throughout summer. The impatiens and 'Vera Jameson' sedum glow with magenta flowers, the 'Happy Returns' daylily with luminous pale yellow.

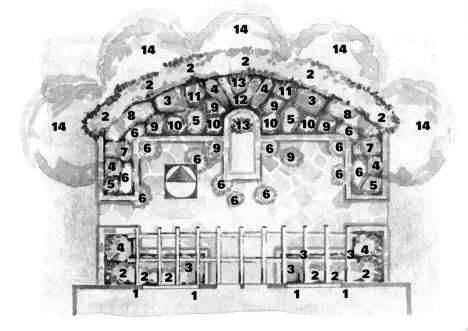

PLANT LIST

1. 'Serotina' honeysuckle, p. 72
2. 'Nikko Blue' bigleaf hydrangea, p. 68
3. 'Pride Rose' impatiens, p. 68
4. Bear's foot hellebore, p. 66
5. 'Blue Danube' Stokes' aster, p. 85
6. Blue plumbago, p. 56
7. 'Blue Spades' columbine, p. 52
8. 'Happy Returns' daylily, p. 67
9. 'Vera Jameson' sedum, p. 85
10. 'Butterfly Blue' pincushion flower, p. 84
11. 'Domino Lime Green' flowering tobacco, p. 76
12. Columbine meadow rue, p. 86
13. Japanese iris, p. 69
14. Kousa dogwood

EVENING TERRACE

Some gardeners find the evening to be the best time to relax and enjoy their flowers. The beauty of white, silver, and pastel hues becomes outstanding at dusk, when pale blooms begin to shimmer in the dimming light. In this garden, the white flowers are intended to be seen at night. Even the creamy honeysuckle and the silvery pastel, cobalt-veined petunia are light enough to be seen by moonlight. The 'Alba' four-o-clock belongs in this garden both for white flowers that open every afternoon as well as delicious scent.

Fragrant plants are some of flower gardening's greatest joys. The design of this garden maximizes the volume of scent reaching people on the terraces. High walls surround the courtyard, making it harder for wind to dissipate the perfume.

Under the open shade of thornless honeylocust trees are plants that bloom from spring through fall. In spring, the beds are filled with especially fragrant varieties of white daffodils, such as 'Rose of May', 'Sinopel', 'Fragrant Breeze', 'Pride of Portugal', and the delicate species pheasant's-eye narcissus. Forget-me-not seed is broadcast in winter to bloom with the daffodils and into the summer. Scented four-o-clock, fragrant white evening primrose, 'Graham Thomas' honeysuckle, and the richly-scented 'Climbing Iceberg' rose on the landing rail bloom all summer. So do the 'Blue-veined Surfinia' petunias cascading from urns topped with the vanilla-rich blooms of white heliotrope. 'Casa Blanca' Oriental lily, white and fragrant, is interplanted with the late-summer blooms of dwarf 'Hummingbird' summersweet. The white butterfly bush, jasmine tobacco, and woodland tobacco also start blooming in midsummer. Moonflower vine twines up into the trees, changing trunks and branches into perfumed trellises. The huge white parasols unfurl in a matter of minutes for a dramatic show each evening—just in time for cocktails.

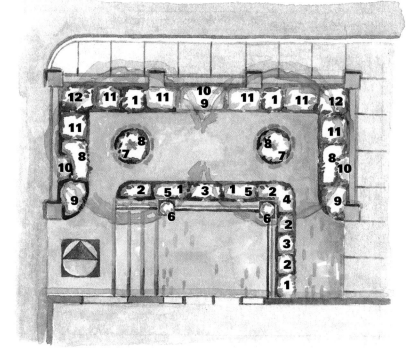

PLANT LIST

1. 'Casa Blanca' Oriental lily, p. 71
2. Fragrant white evening primrose, p. 77
3. 'Iceberg' floribunda rose, p. 82
4. 'Climbing Iceberg' rose, p. 82
5. 'Alba' four-o-clock, p. 74
6. 'Blue-veined Surfinia' petunia, p. 80, cascading from urns, with 'Alba' heliotrope in the center
7. Moonflower, p. 69
8. 'Fragrant Cloud' jasmine tobacco, p. 76
9. Woodland tobacco, p. 76
10. 'Graham Thomas' honeysuckle, p. 72
11. 'Hummingbird' summersweet, p. 58
12. 'White Profusion' butterfly bush, p. 54

EASY FLOWERS: PLANTING AND CARE

Spider flower, dusty miller, flossflower, chrysanthemum, and white geranium sparkle in this neat, sunny border. Most of these flowers are annuals, planted closely to shade out weeds and provide an effect of fullness.

Follow the design principles described in this book—especially those recommending easy, tough, hardworking plants sited where they will be happy—and you will greatly reduce the time and effort needed to enjoy a beautiful, successful flower garden. Nevertheless, where there's a garden, there will be gardening to do. This is a good thing, as gardening is a richly rewarding and enjoyable activity. The trick is to have a beautiful garden where you can do the kind of gardening you most enjoy.

For some people, mowing and caring for large, perfect lawns and clipping neat, formal hedges isn't work at all but a meditative way to relax and enjoy the outdoors. Such people don't mind the long hours and extra expense this kind of gardening entails. Because it doesn't require a lot of thought or knowledge, for them it is easy.

Flower gardening may require a bit more know-how, but with the right techniques and attention, one can enjoy great beauty with far fewer hours and dollars than it takes to care for an expanse of lawn and hedges. And the rewards are more than bountiful color and elegance. Flower gardeners enjoy a connection with the soil, the seasons, and life itself that feeds the soul.

The following pages explain basic techniques and labor-saving shortcuts for planting and maintaining a flower garden with a minimum of fuss. Here is a handy summary of important principles:

USE GOOD TOOLS. With spade, trowel, pruning shears, garden hose, gloves and knee pads, you're ready for about anything. Keep your spade sharp and clean. A bucket of sand is handy to push the spade in for cleaning. Scissor-action pruning shears are best; anvil types tend to crush and damage stems.

APPRECIATE NATURAL PLANT FORMS. The more you impose unnatural or formal shapes on plants, the more time you'll spend.

USE LAWN ONLY WHERE IT PAYS OFF. Lawn is best limited to areas where you really need a plush, wear-resistant surface for foot traffic, play, and lounging. It makes an excellent, low-cost path between sunny beds and borders and is indispensable where children play.

PAY ATTENTION TO EDGING. Deciding where the lawn meets flower bed demands forethought. For some gardeners, edging twice a season with a spade is not too difficult. Others need a more substantial edge to trim against. Probably the most fuss-free edging

of all is a masonry edge, such as soldier-course brick set in mortar. The bricks are set even with the soil, so a mower can run across with no trimming needed.

START WITH GOOD SOIL. Good soil is key to healthy, easy-care flowers. Nearly all soils can be improved with a little organic matter incorporated before planting.

MAKE BEDS THE EASY WAY. In many situations you don't have to dig and till the soil to enjoy beautiful flowers. If your lawn has reasonably good soil underneath and is free of deep-rooted weeds, you can build a flower bed right on top of it without having to remove sod and till the soil (see page 35).

PERFORM MIRACLES WITH MULCH. Proper mulching reduces the amount of time you'll spend watering and weeding, and it conditions the soil for healthier plants. Pages 38–39 summarize the important points to remember.

NIP PROBLEMS IN THE BUD. Get into the habit of walking through the garden daily and paying attention. By catching pests when they are only beginning to be a problem, you'll reduce the need for drastic action.

DON'T WASTE TIME BABYING PLANTS. If a plant doesn't perform, get rid of it and substitute another kind.

DO A LITTLE A LOT. A few minutes in the garden every day saves you from overload down the road.

RELAX. Resist the drive to perfection and learn to enjoy the rough edges of nature. So what if there are a few holes in leaves, a few weeds here or there? You're probably the only one who will notice. Gardens are for pleasure!

Instead of mowing a large lawn, mow a path through a wildflower meadow. The flowers include black-eyed Susan, bee balm, purple coneflower, and prairie coneflower.

START WITH GOOD SOIL

Whether your crop is cut flowers or corn, good soil is key for healthy, lush productivity.

Soil conditions, soil pH, and sufficient levels of nutrients, light, and water are the building blocks of healthy plants. Good standard garden soil contains roughly a third sand, a third silt, and a third clay; it also retains nutrients while allowing air and water to pass through.

Healthy soil contains plenty of organic matter. Organic matter, including leaf mold, compost, and aged manure, breaks down into humus, which aids water retention in sandy, dry areas and loosens soil in dense, wet areas for improved aeration. Nearly all soils can be improved by working a 4- to 6-inch layer of organic matter into the soil with a spade or a tiller. To help your new plants take hold, spade or till a time-release, pelletized fertilizer (such as Osmocote®) and superphosphate or bonemeal into the top 6 inches of soil, following the package directions. If you have heavy, wet clay soil or soil compacted by construction equipment, you can improve its texture by mixing in a generous supply of organic matter when you add the fertilizer.

Soil pH is a gauge of soil acidity on a scale from 0 to 14. Soil at pH 7.0 is neutral. Acid soils are below pH 7.0. Alkaline soils are above 7.0. Most plants thrive between pH 5.5 and 6.5, but some plants, such as rhododendrons, grow best in acid conditions. Others, such as maiden pinks, Russian sage, and most tulips, prefer neutral to slightly alkaline soils. Purchase a soil test kit from a local garden center to determine your soil's pH.

For containers, excellent potting mixes are available at garden centers and nurseries. Some are formulated for special plants, such as azaleas and other acid-loving plants, cacti and succulents, and orchids. Many, however, are all-purpose mixes useful for most garden flowers. Potting mix is sold by the cubic foot. One cubic foot will fill a container 15 inches in diameter and 12 inches deep.

COMPOST

Compost is easy to make at home and benefits the soil. Much household and yard waste can go into the compost pile, which needs air and water to complete the process of decay. Turning the pile provides oxygen for the soil-dwelling microorganisms that eat and digest raw compost, which they excrete as humus, a material high in organic matter and loaded with nutrients.

SAFE INGREDIENTS FOR COMPOST INCLUDE:
- Grass clippings
- Leaves
- Eggshells
- Coffee grounds
- Tea leaves
- Fruit and vegetable scraps
- Benign weeds
- Sawdust
- Chipped branches and prunings
- Wood ash in areas with acid soil
- Shredded newspaper
- Cow or horse manure

AVOID COMPOSTING:
- Feces of meat-eating animals
- Anything cooked in animal fat
- Butter
- Grain-based products
- Invasive plants
- Diseased plant material

EASY FOUR-STEP FLOWER BEDS

After laying out a flower bed with a flexible garden hose, you can establish it at ground level or you can build a raised bed. Both forms of garden bed will provide good soil through which the roots of flowers can grow to support healthy plants.

For a ground-level bed, first cut away the sod by sliding a spade under the roots, or rent a sod stripper. Spread 2 to 6 inches of organic matter, granulated flower fertilizer at the rate recommended on the package label, and pH amendments. Till them into the soil to a depth of 6 to 12 inches.

If your lawn has reasonably good soil and few deep-rooted weeds, you can easily build a small raised bed directly over an area of lawn without removing sod or digging in soil amendments. Because you can fill a raised bed with the soil mix of your choice, the soil in it needs no testing.

Begin by laying landscape fabric over the areas where you want paths. To form the planting beds, lay an 8- to 12-inch layer of sandy loam directly on the lawn. Then mound a 6- to 8-inch layer of compost or aged manure on top of the loam. Smooth the topdressing without incorporating it into the loam. Weight the edges of the landscape fabric with soil and cover the paths with gravel to hold the fabric in place. As you dig each planting hole, mix together the loam and the compost or manure before refilling the hole around the new plant. Do not use peat to mulch the plants; peat is hard to rewet after it has dried.

The purpose of the compost topdressing is to maintain moisture levels, suppress weeds, enrich the soil with organic matter, and keep the garden looking good. Eventually earthworms will combine the compost with the loam. Restore the topdressing by adding 2 to 3 inches of compost or well-rotted manure each year. Where the bed meets lawn, give it a clean line by edging it with a spade.

Step 1: *Outline the bed with a garden hose and lay landscape fabric over paths.*
Step 2: *Spread 8 to 12 inches of sandy loam directly on the lawn where you want the bed.*

Step 3: *Mound 6 to 8 inches of compost on top of the loam and spread it until level and even. Don't worry about mixing it into the loam.*

Step 4: *Weight the edges of the landscape fabric with soil and cover the paths with gravel to hold the fabric in place.*

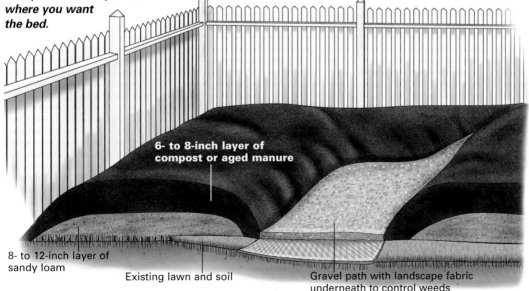

6- to 8-inch layer of compost or aged manure

8- to 12-inch layer of sandy loam

Existing lawn and soil

Gravel path with landscape fabric underneath to control weeds

This raised bed topped with loam and compost drains well, retains moisture, and suppresses weeds. Mix the compost and loam as you dig each planting hole. In a few months, the lawn underneath will break down and earthworms will combine the compost and loam throughout the entire bed.

ACQUIRING PLANTS

Buy blooming specimens when you need a particular color for your garden. Most nursery and garden centers sell plants in plastic pots; a few offer bare-root perennials, including clematis, peonies, and hostas.

Below: A fine web of roots should be visible in the potting soil. If no roots are visible, you're looking at a recent transplant to a bigger pot. Don't buy plants where the roots form a hard, pot-bound mass. Right: Mail-order plants need viable stems and moist, fibrous roots to survive.

Where to buy plants varies from town to town. Local nurseries and garden centers may be more expensive than other outlets, but they usually employ staff to advise you on your purchases. Nurseries tend to grow plants that do well where you live and often propagate plants on site. Some guarantee perennials for a year, which can justify a higher price tag. You can also buy inexpensive plants shipped in bulk to supermarkets and discount stores. Mail-order nurseries usually offer a greater variety of plants that grow well across broad regions of the country, but not as many plants adapted specifically to your region. Depending on the kind of plant, they can arrive at your home either in pots or bare-root. As long as the main stems are viable and the roots are moist and intact, the plants should perform well.

Most annuals are sold in plastic six-packs, although it's sometimes possible to buy larger plants in individual pots or as plugs. Plugs are young plants with small, wedge-shaped root balls that can be transplanted directly into pots or into the ground. A recent entry to the market, they are available more often from mail-order firms but are beginning to be offered at some nurseries and garden centers. Except for growing plants from seed, plugs are the most economical way to fill your garden with flowers. The percentage of success is often less than with more mature transplants, but because they're inexpensive, you can plant plugs more closely and thin them out later.

Perennials are more expensive than annuals because they take more time to mature from cuttings, division, tissue culture, or seed (up to three years). You can sometimes buy perennial plugs, but most nurseries transplant plugs into containers and sell them in larger pots. Some businesses grow perennials in the field, dig them when they're big, and pot them for sale. Perennials raised this way tend to be cold-hardy, having survived winters in your area.

Buy larger, more expensive specimens if you require an immediate effect. But given adequate care, small plants quickly reach the size of bigger plants, so in most circumstances you'll do fine buying small.

POINTERS FOR BUYING PLANTS

■ Buy bushy plants with healthy-looking leaves. Avoid plants with brown, yellow, or crisp leaves.

■ Avoid plants that look tall and spindly.

■ Check plants for pests by examining stems and both sides of the leaves.

■ Try to buy plants before they are blooming, for greatest transplant success. If you need a specific color, however, buy plants in flower or stick to named varieties.

■ A few roots growing through the container bottom are OK; many visible roots are not.

■ If you slip the plant from its pot (ask a salesclerk first), you should see a fine web of roots weaving through the potting medium, not a hard mass of solid roots.

When planting annuals, loosen the outer roots before placing in a hole.

For tough root systems, cut the base into four parts with a sharp knife and set the plant in the hole with the sections slightly spread.

Plant annuals and perennials so the crowns of the plants are at soil level.

PLANTING FLOWERS

Several factors contribute to beautiful flower gardens, including good soil, adequate air circulation, and moisture-retentive mulch. Just as important as planting conditions is the quality of the plants. The best plants are not only healthy but also pest- and disease-resistant.

A key to a vigorous flower garden is leaving sufficient space between plants. Flowering shrubs, perennials, and annuals all benefit from leaves that overlap slightly with their neighbors. In these conditions, the shade of the foliage helps keep the soil moist and supports the establishment of good bacteria that assist the absorption of soil nutrients. Crowding leads to mildew and other fungal diseases that can weaken and even kill affected plants. If you're sowing seeds outdoors, follow the instructions on the packet. For plugs and potted plants, consult the "Gallery of Easy Flowers" (pages 46–91) for mature size. For example, set a plant with a mature width of 8 to 12 inches about 8 to 12 inches away from a similar plant. Setting plants closer together creates a fuller look initially but in the long run makes plants leggy as they reach for the sun.

The maxim "dig a five-dollar hole for a one-dollar plant" holds true when planting a flower garden, because a large area of loosened or amended soil makes it easier for roots to expand and become established. Mix the soil removed from the hole with a like amount of compost or aged manure. Fill the hole halfway with the amended mix. If planting an annual with tender roots, gently loosen the outer roots before setting the plant in the hole. Place the plant in the ground with its crown at soil level. Continue filling the hole with the remaining soil mix. Then mulch and water thoroughly. Water plants daily for a couple of weeks until established.

Follow a similar process for planting perennials, except when preparing to set the plant in the hole. Most perennials have tougher root systems than annuals. For a pot-bound perennial, cut the base of the root ball in fourths with a sharp knife and set the plant with the root quarters slightly spread in the hole. When planting a bare-root perennial, mound the soil mix in the center of the hole, remove dead or damaged roots, and spread the remaining roots evenly over the mound. Use your hands to work soil in and around the roots. Fill the hole with the remaining soil mix, keeping the plant's crown at soil level.

PLANTING BARE-ROOT PLANTS

Many perennials and shrubs acquired from mail-order firms are shipped as dormant, bare-root plants. Some retail nurseries also offer bare-root plants in early spring. Inspect plants to make sure they're dormant and not pushing new growth. The root system should be moist and fresh-looking with a minimum of broken or blackened roots. Return plants with broken or dried-out roots. Remove plants from packaging right away and plant or, if you must, store plants in damp sawdust or bark for up to a week.

When planting, prune rose roots by one-third or more. Soak roots in water for several hours before planting. Don't soak or heavily prune perennials except to remove damaged or very long roots. Dig a hole large enough for the full root span, and make a cone of soil over which you will spread the roots. Set grafted roses with the top root 1 inch below ground; for other plants, follow instructions from the nursery. Remove air pockets by working soil between the roots with your hands, then finish filling the hole and water in the plant.

FERTILIZING YOUR PLANTS

Flowers densely planted in containers will stay healthy and bloom profusely when regularly fertilized with a high phosphorus and potash blend. These lush pots are filled with verbena, white geranium, lantana, 'Victoria' salvia, and 'Lady in Red' Texas sage.

Different plants have different feeding requirements, but most need some extra nutrients to stay healthy. Heavy blooming, sun-loving annuals require more feeding than foliage plants grown in shade.

The three main elements of plant nutrition are nitrogen, phosphorus, and potassium, depicted in order as N-P-K on fertilizer labels. Nitrogen is necessary for healthy leaves, phosphorus for abundant flowers, and potassium (potash) for sturdy roots. Fertilizer labels express the balance of these nutrients by numerical ratios. To encourage leaf growth, use a ratio with higher nitrogen content (20-10-5, for example). To promote lavish fruiting and flowering, use a ratio with higher phosphorus and potash (such as 10-52-10).

Moreover, for nutrient absorption to occur, soil pH must be neutral (from 6.5 to 7.5 on a 14-point scale) or slightly acid (5.5 to 6.5). Some fertilizers are designed to acidify soil. To make soil more alkaline, apply lime according to package directions.

Feeding plants in warm climates is as easy as applying one dose of time-release fertilizer each spring. Because sulfur-coated time-release fertilizers do not reach their maximum release rate until soil temperatures reach 75 degrees F, Osmocote® or liquid fertilizers are better choices for cool-spring climates. To apply liquid fertilizers, use a watering can or a hose fitted with a y-connector and a short siphon hose leading into the pail.

Use houseplant fertilizer sticks to feed baskets and containers that are out of reach. Sticks last about two months and are quick and easy to replace. Simply follow the package directions, inserting them into the soil when you plant containerized annuals.

A y-connector is used to siphon concentrated soluble fertilizer from a bucket and dilute it to the proper strength when watering plants.

MULCH: THE MIRACLE WORKER

Mulch benefits the flower garden. It smothers weeds, the bane of every gardener who has watched them compete with desirable plants for moisture, airspace, and soil nutrients. Mulch also saves time spent weeding and watering.

In summer, mulch keeps soil moist and cool, because it's not exposed to the drying effects of the hot sun.

In winter, mulch blankets the soil, maintaining its warmth and preventing shallow-rooted plants and newly planted shrubs and perennials from heaving during cycles of freezing and thawing. Mulch increases the movement of earthworms in the soil. As organic mulch decomposes, these garden heroes eat and digest it, excreting

organic matter which increases the amount of humus in the soil and improves its nutrient content.

Because organic mulch is eventually incorporated into the soil, it's necessary to renew it every year or two by spreading a 1- to 2-inch layer on top of the bed. Mulch thicker than 3 to 4 inches may encourage nesting rodents. Also,

Wood chips offer an attractive way to suppress weeds and maintain warmth and soil moisture.

Ground bark is readily available in nearly all regions. It provides good protection but breaks down quickly.

WATERING YOUR PLANTS

Remember to plant flowers with similar cultural needs together. Then tailor the frequency of watering to the needs of the plants in the beds. Seedlings and recent transplants need frequent watering until established, at least daily for about two weeks or more. Most plants need watering during a drought. Potted plants in a sunny, windy location may need watering more than once a day.

Once your plants are established, a slow, deep watering is better than a daily spritz. Short bursts of water promote shallow rooting; deep watering promotes deep rooting. Plants with deep root systems are better able to withstand drought, because their roots can search for moisture far into the ground.

Encourage moisture retention in the soil and reduce the need for watering by mulching and incorporating organic matter. A 3-inch layer of organic mulch slows evaporation by cooling the soil on hot days. Increasing the content of organic matter in sandy or gravely soil enhances its capacity to retain moisture.

Methods for delivering extra water range from inexpensive but time-consuming hand watering with hoses, soaker hoses, and sprinklers to the more high-tech solutions of automatic overhead or drip irrigation.

Two simple items are handy for watering flower gardens: the watering wand and the soaker hose. Long-necked wands are excellent for reaching containers in out-of-the-way locations, as well as watering beds of delicate flowers and seedlings with a gentle yet efficient spray. Soaker hoses apply water gently and deeply. If you buy several and leave them in place for the entire season, you won't have to move them. Simply attach a garden hose to each, one by one, as you work elsewhere in the garden.

Bubblers keep foliage dry while watering a specific plant or series of plants using trenches to direct water where it's needed. Sprinklers, on the other hand, simulate rainfall by wetting the entire plant from above. The best time for overhead watering is in the morning, when sunlight gently dries the leaves. Afternoon sun is hot and intense; leaves dry fast, but it doesn't take long for water droplets to act like tiny magnifying glasses and cause scorching.

Drip irrigation reduces water consumption, an especially welcome benefit in parts of the country where water is scarce and expensive. Water slowly seeps through narrow emitters, giving nearby plants a deep and thorough soaking over time with minimal evaporation.

Whether overhead or drip, automatic irrigation systems are initially costly but save a lot of time and work over the years. Ortho's *All About Sprinklers and Drip Systems* provides instructions for you to design and install a system yourself.

This watering ring, made especially for containers, directs little jets of water at the base of plants.

Low-spraying automatic heads water plants without wetting their leaves.

Watering hanging pots is easy with a handheld wand.

keep organic mulches about 1 inch away from flower stems and 6 inches away from the woody stems of shrubs and the trunks of trees. It is important to keep mulch away from the crowns of perennials. Closer applications may cause plants to rot and create habitats for pests.

Organic mulches range from compost, chopped leaves, newsprint, and chipped or shredded bark to grass clippings, sawdust, aged manure, pine needles, salt hay, and evergreen boughs. Be careful when using straw, hay, compost, and aged manure, because they sometimes introduce weed seeds into the garden. Inorganic mulches include natural materials such as gravel, seashells, and marble dust as well as synthetic products such as landscape fabric and black plastic. Plastic mulches are best suited to the vegetable garden, where they warm the soil in early spring. Landscape fabric is good for shrub borders, where it can be cut to open around each plant or follow irregular bed lines. Hide the fabric under a layer of shredded bark or some other more attractive mulch.

Pine needles make an excellent acidic mulch with a delicate texture and honey gold color.

Shredded pine bark knits together to stay in place through wind and rain.

SEASONAL MAINTENANCE

Prioritizing maintenance tasks makes sense for busy gardeners. At the top of the list is making sure your plants stay healthy so they can fulfill their floral destiny. Take a daily walk around the garden to enjoy the blooms and check for garden problems.

WATERING: If plants are wilting, ensure their survival by watering them deeply right away. Always provide extra water to new and established plantings during times of drought.

SPOTTING PESTS AND DISEASES: Catch pests and diseases early. If you spot a severely disease- or pest-ridden plant, pull it out and toss it in the garbage can. Do not add it to the compost pile, where pests and diseases may live on to infect other plant material. Similarly, collect unhealthy leaves or branches from the ground and put them in the garbage.

For diagnosing and choosing treatments for pests and diseases, *The Ortho Problem Solver* is an excellent reference. Most garden centers and nurseries keep a copy handy for your reference. Follow package directions carefully when applying pesticides and fungicides.

STAKING: Some flowering plants collapse during storms or from excess height or weight. You can avoid the battered look by staking plants early in the season and restaking them if necessary as they grow. Popular staking methods include pea staking, metal hoops, and bamboo stakes with string. Pea stakes suit plants such as shasta daisy, which forms broad, leggy clumps as it grows. For pea stakes, use dried butterfly bush branches or other sturdy twigs saved from the annual early-spring pruning. Insert them deep in the ground so the staked perennial can disguise them as it grows. Hoops, especially those with grow-through grids, are useful for staking peonies and other top-heavy plants.

WEEDING: Don't let weeding get you down. Although weeds compete for space, moisture, and nutrients with your garden plants, a weed here and there will not destroy the health or overall appearance of your garden. Beware, however, of letting weeds grow so rampant that they overtake the flowers. It's easier to pull a few weeds each day on a garden stroll than it is to face a yard of unchecked weeds once a month.

DIVIDING: When clump-forming perennials such as hardy geranium and chrysanthemum begin to die out in the center, dig them up and divide them into several smaller plants, discarding the middle. Divide spring-blooming perennials in summer and early fall, and summer or fall bloomers in early spring.

PINCHING AND DISBUDDING: Removing the growth tips off leggy shoots yields shorter, bushier plants with more flowers. With perennials such as chrysanthemum, you can increase the blooms and delay their onset by pinching off growing points in late spring and again in midsummer. With annuals such as petunia, pinch a third of the stems by two-thirds each week or two for abundant bloom.

After flowers have bloomed, prune flower stalks and foliage that looks brown, streaked, or withered. If the leaves look bad, trim them to 6 inches for uniformity, or cut single leaves at different angles to simulate Mother Nature. Do not compost these cuttings because they may be diseased.

EASY FLOWERS THAT RESPOND TO DEADHEADING

Azalea	Marigold
Balloon flower	Mullein
Bee balm	Petunia
Blanket flower	Pincushion flower
Butterfly weed	Pot marigold
Catmint	Rhododendron
Coral bells	Rose
Coreopsis	Sage; salvia
Cosmos	Shasta daisy
Daylily (reblooming)	Snapdragon
False sunflower	Spiderwort
Flossflower	Stokes' aster
Garden phlox	Sunflower
Geranium; pelargonium	Sweet alyssum
	Sweet William
Japanese spirea	Treasure flower
Larkspur	Yarrow
Lavender	Yellow corydalis
Maiden pink	Zinnia

DEADHEADING: After a plant flowers, it marshalls energy for reproduction by setting seed. Deadheading, or removing faded flowers, sends that energy into flower production or more vigorous roots. Most annuals experience increased flowering after deadheading. Perennials that bloom on leaf-bearing stems will also keep producing flowers when deadheaded. Cutting back perennials such as 'Dropmore' catmint and 'Moonbeam' coreopsis promotes a second flush of flowers and a denser habit later in summer. Many perennials, including salvia, garden phlox, pincushion flower, and purple coneflower, look tidier and fuller when you remove dead blossoms. Deadhead plants with basal foliage and leafless flower stems to clean them up and direct their energy into establishing vigorous roots. To deadhead plants with basal foliage, snip the bottom of the flower stems and add the discards to the compost pile.

Leave plants with interesting seed heads in the garden. Some, such as purple coneflowers, are favored by birds; others add form and mass to the winter garden. Keep seed heads of ornamental grasses, money plant, 'Autumn Joy' sedum, and other garden plants with ornamental elements in your yard until early spring, when you can cut them down before they put on new growth. Remove annuals after they've been killed by frost, and cut back perennials whose forms do not persist.

If you're interested in saving seeds for the following year, cut a few ripe seedpods or seed heads, dry them, and store them in labeled and dated envelopes (see page 42).

Wait until early spring to cut back 'Autumn Joy' sedum and ornamental grasses, because their handsome leaves and seed heads continue to look good throughout winter.

FLOWERS WITH ATTRACTIVE WINTER SEEDS AND FRUITS

Anise hyssop
'Autumn Joy' sedum
Black-eyed Susan
Butterfly bush
Butterfly weed
Clematis
Joe-Pye weed
Miscanthus
Money plant
Mullein
Oakleaf hydrangea
Peegee hydrangea
Purple coneflower
Roses (some)

WHEN TO PRUNE FLOWERING SHRUBS

A shrub's flowering season determines its pruning time. Prune shrubs that flower in spring on old wood right after flowering. Fall or winter pruning would destroy buds that would bloom the next spring.

Prune summer-flowering shrubs after flowering, or in late fall or early spring before growth begins. If you wait until growth starts in spring, you'll remove the current season's flowers. Cut back butterfly bush to 12 inches in early spring so you can enjoy its seed heads in winter and use the cut branches as pea stakes in spring. Hard-pruning butterfly bush and some roses forfeits many smaller blooms for fewer but larger blooms.

Deadheading lilacs within three weeks of blooming results in increased flowering the following spring. Deadheading after three weeks may improve the shrub's appearance but will not noticeably affect future flowering. Snap off faded flowers of rhododendrons to promote increased flowering the next spring.

MAKING MORE: BASIC PROPAGATION

When sowing seeds indoors, make sure you are prepared. Use fresh seed when possible, and clean all equipment before you begin. For a high rate of germination, follow light and temperature suggestions for each type of seed. Good air circulation and regular watering prevent most problems.

Growing plants from seed, cuttings, and division saves money. It also lets you grow exactly the plants you want. Just as vital, propagating plants can satisfy spiritual needs for nurture, beauty, and increase that lie deep within us.

SEED

Some seeds germinate best when sown directly in the garden. For instance, you can sow annual poppies and pot marigolds outdoors in fall in warm-climate gardens and in early spring in cool areas. Tree mallow and love-in-a-mist prefer to be sown outdoors in early spring; nasturtiums, cosmos, sunflower, and moss rose require waiting until after the last frost for outdoor sowing.

Read the seed packet, because some seeds have special light and temperature requirements for germination. Packets also list the average number of days to germination to help you time sowing dates. Hardiness rankings on packets include HP (hardy perennial; germinating seeds do best when overwintered outdoors), HA (hardy annual; frost-tolerant seeds to sow in fall for spring bloom), and HHA (half-hardy annual; frost-tender seeds to sow in spring for bloom the same season).

To start seeds indoors by a window, fill some clean pots with a seed-starting soil mix or with potting soil mixed with vermiculite for excellent drainage. Read the seed packet or consult a book to see if your seeds need light or darkness to germinate, because that affects the amount of soil you'll sprinkle on top of them. Usually you'll cover seeds with three times their depth in soil. To grow large numbers of seeds, you'll need grow-lights, heat pads, and seed trays or flats.

Keep seed trays and pots evenly moist. Adequate air circulation is important to control damping-off, mildew, aphids, and mites. Sometimes installing a small oscillating fan is enough to avert these problems. After germination, thin seedlings by cutting stems off with nail scissors.

When the seedlings develop two or three true leaves, transplant them into 4-inch pots filled with light-textured potting soil. Lift them from flats and plug trays by their leaves, not by their easily damaged stems. Move the transplants farther from the light source for a few days and mist them three or four times a day. Feed weekly with transplant fertilizer or a regular plant food at half strength. Transform leggy seedlings into compact, bushy plants by pinching growing tips or new leaves every week to 10 days.

As warm weather nears, harden off new plants for life outdoors by placing them in a shaded, sheltered space in the garden for a few hours daily. Increase exposure to sunlight each day, bringing the plants indoors at night. The process takes about two weeks for hardy plants and three or more weeks for tropicals.

COLLECTING SEEDS FROM YOUR OWN PLANTS

To turn this year's annuals into next year's flowers, let several particularly fine blooms on healthy plants set seed after the plants have flowered. Gather the seed heads or seedpods when they are brown and starting to split, place them in a clean paper bag or an envelope, and keep them in a warm, dry place until dried (usually several days to a week). Gently shake the seeds onto clean paper, remove any debris, and package them in brown coin envelopes labeled with the name of the plant and the date. Store the envelopes in a cool drawer or cabinet with low humidity to maintain the seeds' viability. Seed saved from named hybrid cultivars often do not come true, but instead resemble one of the cultivar's parents. Non-hybrid plants grown from seed usually look like the parent.

CUTTINGS

Many plants can be increased by taking stem or tip cuttings. Midsummer tip cuttings of fast-rooting perennials such as garden phlox and sage will give you a lot of plants quickly. Other plants easy to root from cuttings include geranium, oregano, moss rose, verbena, sedum, butterfly bush, climbing hydrangea, and blue plumbago.

■ To make stem cuttings, remove a few sturdy, unflowered side shoots 5 to 6 inches long, dip in rooting hormone with fungicide, and insert, cut side down, into sandy soil.

■ For tip cuttings, take the top 3 to 4 inches of unflowered stems, choosing pieces that are flexible but substantive. Dip in rooting hormone and insert, cut side down, into sandy soil. Cover the cuttings with muslin to provide shade and conserve moisture.

To divide rhizomatous plants such as bearded iris, first break apart the clump by hand. Then cut the new rhizomes off the clump, throwing out old material. Cut off the ends and dip the cuts in fungicide. Cut back the leaves to 4 to 6 inches and roots by one-third.

DIVISION

An easy way to propagate perennials is by division, a process that not only multiplies the number of plants but also keeps them vigorous. If a perennial that once bloomed heavily bears few flowers or meager stems, or if it has died out at the center of the clump, division may be what's needed to reinvigorate its growth. Hosta, daylily, and Siberian iris are vigorous, easy-to-grow plants with dense root systems that may benefit from dividing every three years. On the other hand, some perennials require no dividing unless they outgrow their location. For success with division, follow these guidelines:

■ In cold climates, divide and replant perennials in spring or early fall. In warmer areas, divide in fall. Divide early bloomers such as Shasta daisy late in the season and late bloomers such as asters and obedient plant in early spring. Most perennials are so tough, however, that you can divide them with success whenever you have time.

■ To divide a perennial, dig up the mother plant and shake or knock off excess dirt.

■ Separate daylilies, hostas, and other clump-forming plants that produce multiple crowns with back-to-back garden forks.

■ Slice through smaller perennials such as coral bells and coreopsis with a sharp knife.

■ Use the cutting edge of a spade to divide bee balm and other spreading perennials into smaller sections.

■ Chop miscanthus and perennials with exceptionally tough roots with a hatchet.

■ Break off the rhizomes (thick storage roots) of plants such as canna, keeping a growth point or viable tuft of foliage with each root.

■ Throw out woody roots from the center of the plant, and replant the young, vital shoots.

The easiest way to divide daylilies, which have a dense, fibrous root mass, is to use back-to-back garden forks to work the roots apart. To make small pieces, use your hands or the edge of a sharp spade. Replant healthy root sections with vigorous new shoots.

A sharp knife works well when dividing small perennials. Make sure to clean the knife with bleach before starting, to avoid contaminating the new plants with soilborne diseases. Discard the center of the old plant, which tends to lack vigor. Plant divisions at the same depth as the mother plant.

MAINTENANCE CALENDAR

WINTER

- ■ Evaluate your garden's performance over the past year.
- ■ Read gardening books.
- ■ Design next season's beds.
- ■ Study catalogs and order plants and seeds.
- ■ Avoid excessive use of de-icing salt near flower beds.
- ■ If possible, avoid walking on frozen grass, which may damage the blades.
- ■ Check your garden for winter damage.
- ■ Press frost-heaved plants back into the ground during winter thaws.
- ■ In the North, start seeds with long germination periods indoors.
- ■ In the South, set out primroses, maiden pinks, and violas.
- ■ Take cuttings of geraniums (*Pelargonium*) to plant in late spring.

SPRING

- ■ In the North, remove mulch from the base of perennials and roses as weather warms.
- ■ Fertilize spring-blooming bulbs when they emerge.
- ■ Plant cold-tolerant annuals (pansies, violas, forget-me-nots).
- ■ Cut back ornamental grasses and perennials kept for winter interest before new growth begins.
- ■ Test the soil in your flower beds.
- ■ Clean up ground covers.
- ■ Prepare established flower beds by removing dead plant material, weeding, and tilling soil.
- ■ Top-dress beds with compost or aged manure.
- ■ Create new flower beds.
- ■ Harden off hardy and half-hardy seedlings.
- ■ Divide perennials.
- ■ Plant new perennials.
- ■ Mulch beds as needed.
- ■ Plant bare-root roses as soon as you can work the soil.
- ■ Prune spring-flowering shrubs such as lilac, rhododendron, and forsythia after bloom.
- ■ Where necessary, repot and fertilize plants in containers.
- ■ Set out tender annuals after the final frost.
- ■ Move potted plants outdoors after the last frost.
- ■ Stake top-heavy and tall perennials.
- ■ Sow annual and perennial seeds.

SUMMER

Pull a few weeds as you stroll through the garden.

Give extra water to new and established flowers and shrubs during dry spells.

Fertilize container plants.

Pinch back asters, cosmos, zinnias, salvias, and chrysanthemums to encourage branching and more blooms.

Divide and replant bearded iris.

Divide daylilies after they've bloomed.

Remove yellowed daffodil foliage.

Divide clumps of spring-flowering bulbs with meager blooms.

Cut early-blooming perennials such as catmint and spiderwort to the ground to promote new growth.

■ Deadhead annuals to extend flowering.

■ Train vines.

Cut down hollyhocks after blooming or before they grow rangy.

Plant fall-blooming bulbs.

FALL

■ Divide most perennials.

■ Divide peonies before the first frost.

■ Pull out dead annuals and add them to the compost pile.

■ In warm climates, sow annual poppies, larkspur, and pot marigolds for next year's garden.

■ In cold climates, dig up tender bulbs, tubers, and corms after the leaves have died.

■ Plant spring-blooming bulbs. You can plant daffodils until the ground freezes.

■ Move houseplants indoors; check carefully for insects before bringing in.

■ Dig and pot tender ornamental grasses.

■ Flag the location of perennials such as butterfly weed, balloon flower, blue plumbago, and rose mallow that emerge late in spring.

■ Divide Oriental poppies.

■ Cut back tops of perennials that are not being kept for winter interest.

■ Apply a winter mulch such as pine boughs to perennial gardens after the ground has frozen.

■ Force paper-white narcissus for bloom indoors.

GALLERY OF EASY FLOWERS

Whether in a pot or in the ground, it's hard to beat geraniums and daylilies for vigor and long-blooming performance. Use this gallery to find the top-rated cultivars of each. You'll find more on geraniums on page 79, and daylilies on page 67.

Several criteria went into choosing the annuals, perennials, and shrubs for this gallery. Try to keep these checkpoints in mind when shopping for other easy flowers. Easy flowers should be:

LONG-BLOOMING: Flowers that bloom for at least six weeks maximize their impact on the garden and make the money you spend on plants worthwhile. In fact, the smaller your property, the harder each plant needs to work.

INTERESTING IN MORE THAN ONE SEASON: In many cases, the plants in this gallery have handsome foliage and form that add to their garden appeal even when the plants are at rest and not blooming. Some have fall color or a striking winter presence.

AVAILABLE: The plants listed in this gallery are easy to find in most parts of the country. On page 91, we list mail-order sources for varieties your nursery might not carry.

PEST-RESISTANT: In spite of tender care, some plants succumb to insects such as whitefly, mites, beetles, and other pests of the growing season. Where possible, we've chosen varieties that garden pests are likely to ignore.

DISEASE-RESISTANT: Hand in hand with pest resistance is disease resistance. Healthy plants with undamaged leaves and stems survive best. We've chosen varieties for many garden circumstances and described cultivars that have inbred resistance to disease.

LOW-MAINTENANCE: Look for plants that produce beautiful blooms yet do not require constant pruning and feeding. You'll find in this gallery that even some notoriously high-demand plants such as roses have easy, dependable varieties that require little care.

VIGOROUS YET EASY TO CONTROL: Most plants in this gallery have the perfect balance of vigorous health yet restrained growth habit that makes them easy to keep in bounds. Yet there's a place for plants that spread quickly—where you need big coverage fast, or where contained beds can check growth. When we have included such plants, we warn you of their romping habits.

ENTRIES PACKED WITH INFORMATION

Profile and size: Size shown is the average of a typical species when grown under optimum conditions. For perennials, the size shown is by the second or third season of growth; for annuals, by the peak of season; for shrubs, by the fourth season of growth. The width shown should be used as a guide for spacing.

At-a-glance features: Plant type is followed by USDA hardiness zones for perennials and chief attractions of each plant.

Culture: This important section describes conditions for optimum growth and basic care instructions.

Scientific name and pronunciation: Entries are alphabetized by Latin name.

Common name: Each entry prominently displays the common name.

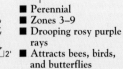

ECHINACEA PURPUREA
eh-ki-NAY-see-a pur-PUR-ee-a
Purple coneflower

3'
2'

- Perennial
- Zones 3–9
- Drooping rosy purple rays
- Attracts bees, birds, and butterflies

'Magnus' purple coneflower

This wildflower, native to the North American prairie, attracts attention for its striking blooms from summer to fall. It ranges from 2 to 4 feet tall and produces flowers from 4 to 6 inches wide.

USES: Purple coneflower belongs in beds and borders and makes an ideal addition to meadow gardens. Sturdy stems and an attractive form make it good for cutting. Minus the rays, which are short-lived when cut, the long-lasting central cone is a welcome addition to both fresh and dried arrangements.

CULTURE: This tough landscape plant needs little attention once established. It prefers full sun and well-drained, average garden soil. Purple coneflower is both drought- and heat-tolerant. When grown in too much shade or too-rich soil, it may flop and need staking.

RECOMMENDED VARIETIES: 'Bravado', 4 feet high, has 6-inch flowers with wide, horizontal petals. 'Magnus', a vivid purplish-red, also has horizontal rays. 'White Swan', 2 to 3 feet tall, has pure white rays. 'Bright Star' has rosy pink rays and bronze cones.

Photograph: Each listing includes a color photograph of a representative specimen identified by cultivar, when appropriate.

Introduction: A brief description outlines why you might want to grow this plant.

Uses: Here you'll find suggestions for where to situate the plant for best effect.

Recommended varieties: The best cultivars and related species for easy care are listed in this section.

The "Gallery of Easy Flowers" has been carefully designed to pack a lot of detail into a condensed space. So that you can get the most out of the information provided, this diagram shows how the gallery is organized for each entry.

WHAT'S IN A NAME?

Plant names come in many forms. Most garden plants have common names inspired by notable characteristics and a touch of whimsy. Love-lies-bleeding, love-in-a-mist, and forget-me-not are three of the many garden plants with quaint and appealing names.

Common names can be fun and are often easier to pronounce and remember than botanical names. But they also are the source of a lot of confusion in the plant world. Many plants have several common names, often differing regionally. Sometimes two completely different plants have the same common name. And many plants have no common name at all.

Each garden plant, however, has a unique scientific name derived from botanical Latin. Every plant belongs to a group with members that have

similar features. This group, known as the genus, contains smaller, more narrowly defined groups, known as species. A cultivar, or cultivated variety, is a selection of a species with unusual attributes, or a hybrid bred by crossing two different plants, often two species.

Acquire the correct plant at nurseries and garden centers by looking for a label with the plant's genus, species, and cultivar. *Dicentra eximia* 'Snowdrift', for example, is a superior white fringed bleeding heart that blooms all summer. If you just ask for "white bleeding heart," you might mistakenly buy *Dicentra spectabilis* 'Alba', a white-blooming selection of the old-fashioned Japanese bleeding heart that only blooms for about 2 weeks in late spring.

This plant is a hybrid between two species with the botanical name of Geranium 'Johnson's Blue'. *Its common name is geranium.*

The common name of this completely different plant is also geranium (pelargonium in the West). Its botanical name is Pelargonium × hortorum.

BLOOM SEASON CHART

Use this chart to help you plan overlapping seasons of bloom for color all year. Because the flowers are listed in order of bloom, you can easily see at a glance which ones bloom together, which bloom in succession, and which bloom for extra-long times. Remember that any bloom chart will be only a rough guide, as bloom seasons can differ according to the region, the weather, microclimates, and cultivars. Blue bars represent bloom seasons; orange bars represent fall foliage and fruit.

(■ = bloom season; ▨ = fall foliage and fruit)

Plant Name	Spr. E	Spr. M	Spr. L	Sum. E	Sum. M	Sum. L	Fall E	Fall M	Fall L	Win. E	Win. M	Win. L
Hellebores (Helleborus spp.)	■	■	■									■
Daffodil (Narcissus hybrids)	■	■										
Tulip (Tulipa hybrids)	■	■										
Forget-me-not (Myosotis sylvatica)	■	■										
Pansy and viola (Viola spp.)	■	■	■								■	■
Sweet violet (Viola odorata)	■	■										
New Zealand tea-tree (Leptospermum scoparium)	■	■		■								
California poppy (Eschscholzia californica)		■	■	■								
Azalea and rhododendron (Rhododendron spp.)		■	■	■								
Fringed bleeding heart (Dicentra eximia)		■	■	■	■	■						
Annual poppy (Papaver spp.)		■	■	■								
Columbine (Aquilegia spp.)		■	■	■								
Clematis (Clematis spp.)				■	■	■	■					
Pot marigold (Calendula officinalis)				■	■	■	■					
Arkansas amsonia (Amsonia hubrechtii)				■		▨						
Shasta daisy (Chrysanthemum × leucanthemum)				■	■							
Yellow corydalis (Corydalis lutea)				■	■							
Foxglove (Digitalis purpurea)				■	■							
Coral bells (Heuchera spp.)				■	■							
Siberian iris (Iris sibirica)				■								
Spotted dead nettle (Lamium maculatum)				■								
Perennial flax (Linum perenne)				■	■							
Money plant (Lunaria annua)				■		▨						
Catmint (Nepeta × faassenii)				■	■	■						
Peony (Paeonia hybrids)				■								
Oriental poppy (Papaver orientale)				■								
Soapwort (Saponaria spp.)					■							
Spiderwort (Tradescantia spp.)				■	■							
Columbine meadow rue (Thalictrum aquilegiifolium)				■								

Plant Name	Spr. E	Spr. M	Spr. L	Sum. E	Sum. M	Sum. L	Fall E	Fall M	Fall L	Win. E	Win. M	Win. L
Snapdragon (Antirrhinum majus)				■	■	■						
Larkspur (Consolida ambigua)				■	■							
Dwarf morning glory (Convolvulus tricolor)				■	■							
Sweet William (Dianthus barbatus)				■	■							
Petunia (Petunia hybrids)				■	■	■						
Rose (Rosa spp. and hybrids)				■	■	■	▨					
Hollyhock (Alcea rosea)				■	■	■						
Hybrid sage (Salvia × sylvestris)				■	■	■						
Maiden pink (Dianthus deltoides)				■	■							
Pincushion flower (Scabiosa columbaria)				■	■	■	■					
Rock rose (Cistus spp.)				■								
Fleabane (Erigeron spp. and hybrids)				■	■							
Bee balm (Monarda didyma)				■	■							
'Stella de Oro' daylily (Hemerocallis 'Stella de Oro')					■	■	■					
Trumpet honeysuckle (Lonicera sempervirens)				■	■		▨					
Blanket flower (Gaillardia × grandiflora)					■	■						
Wax begonia (Begonia semperflorens-cultorum)					■	■						
Sweet alyssum (Lobularia maritima)					■	■						
Astilbe (Astilbe spp.)					■	▨						
Nolana (Nolana paradoxa)					■	■						
Flossflower (Ageratum houstonianum)					■	■						
Butterfly weed (Asclepias tuberosa)					■	▨						
White gaura (Gaura lindheimeri)					■	■	■					
Lantana (Lantana camara)					■	■						
English lavender (Lavandula angustifolia)					■	■						
Lily (Lilium hybrids)					■							
Sea lavender (Limonium latifolium)					■							
Japanese spirea (Spiraea japonica)					■							
Mullein (Verbascum spp.)					■	■		■	■			

Plant Name	Spr E	Spr M	Spr L	Sum E	Sum M	Sum L	Fall E	Fall M	Fall L	Win E	Win M	Win L
Vinca (*Catharanthus roseus*)				■	■	■	■					
Nasturtium (*Tropaeolum majus*)				■	■	■						
Geranium (*Pelargonium × hortorum*)				■	■	■						
Mandevilla (*Mandevilla × amabilis*)				■	■	■						
Evening primrose (*Oenothera* spp.)				■	■							
Oregano (*Origanum* spp.)				■	■							
Bush cinquefoil (*Potentilla fruticosa*)				■	■	■						
Love-lies-bleeding (*Amaranthus caudatus*)				■	■	▒						
Gazania (*Gazania rigens*)				■	■	■						
Globe amaranth (*Gomphrena globosa*)				■	■	■						
Strawflower (*Helichrysum bracteatum*)				■	■	■						
Impatiens (*Impatiens* spp.)				■	■							
Flowering tobacco (*Nicotiana* spp.)				■	■							
Love-in-a-mist (*Nigella damascena*)				■	■							
Moss rose (*Portulaca grandiflora*)				■	■	■						
Sage; salvia (*Salvia* spp.)				■	■							
Scarlet runner bean (*Phaseolus coccineus*)				■	■	■						
Creeping zinnia (*Sanvitalia procumbens*)				■	■	■						
Marigold (*Tagetes* hybrids)				■	■	■						
Black-eyed Susan vine (*Thunbergia alata*)				■	■	■						
Common yarrow (*Achillea millefolium*)				■								
Daylily (*Hemerocallis* hybrids)				■	■	■						
Smokebush (*Cotinus coggygria*)				■	■	▒						
Verbena (*Verbena* spp.)				■	■	■						
Spider flower (*Cleome hassleriana*)				■	■	■						
Cosmos (*Cosmos* spp.)				■	■	■						
Zinnia (*Zinnia* spp. and hybrids)				■	■	■						
Coreopsis (*Coreopsis* spp.)				■	■	■						
'Autumn Joy' sedum (*Sedum* 'Autumn Joy')				■	■	■	■	▒				
Agapanthus (*Agapanthus* spp.)				■	■							
Stokes' aster (*Stokesia laevis*)				■	■							
Ornamental pepper (*Capsicum annuum*)				■	■	■						
Cockscomb (*Celosia argentea* var. *cristata*)				■	■	■						

Plant Name	Spr E	Spr M	Spr L	Sum E	Sum M	Sum L	Fall E	Fall M	Fall L	Win E	Win M	Win L
Hyacinth bean (*Dolichos lablab*)				■	■							
Four-o-clock (*Mirabilis jalapa*)				■	■							
Purple coneflower (*Echinacea purpurea*)				■	■	▒	▒					
Butterfly bush (*Buddleia davidii*)				■	■							
Canna (*Canna* hybrids)					■	■						
Oakleaf hydrangea (*Hydrangea quercifolia*)				■	■	▒						
Blue plumbago (*Ceratostigma plumbaginoides*)					■	■	▒					
Russian sage (*Perovskia atriplicifolia*)					■	■						
Morning glory, moonflower, cypress vine (*Ipomoea* spp.)					■	■						
Sunflower (*Helianthus annuus*)					■	▒						
Tree mallow (*Lavatera trimestris*)					■	■						
Hardy amaryllis (*Lycoris squamigera*)					■							
Black-eyed Susan (*Rudbeckia* spp.)					■	■	▒	▒				
False sunflower (*Heliopsis helianthoides* var. *scabra*)					■							
Rose of Sharon (*Hibiscus syriacus*)					■							
Rose mallow (*Hibiscus moscheutos*)					■							
Bigleaf hydrangea (*Hydrangea macrophylla*)					■							
Garden phlox (*Phlox paniculata*)					■							
Balloon flower (*Platycodon grandiflorus*)					■	■	▒					
Helen's flower (*Helenium autumnale*)					■	■						
Mexican sunflower (*Tithonia rotundifolia*)					■							
Golden lace (*Patrinia scabiosifolia*)					■							
Anise hyssop (*Agastache foeniculum*)					■							
Miscanthus (*Miscanthus sinensis*)							■	■	■			
Chaste tree (*Vitex agnus-castus*)						■						
Joe-Pye weed (*Eupatorium purpureum*)							■	■	■			
Summersweet (*Clethra alnifolia*)						■	▒					
Obedient plant (*Physostegia virginiana*)						■						
Boltonia (*Boltonia asteroides*)							■	■				
Lavender mist meadow rue (*Thalictrum rochebrunianum*)						■						
Frikart's aster (*Aster × frikartii*)						■						

ACHILLEA SPP.

a-KIL-lee-a

Yarrow

'Moonshine' yarrow

- ■ Perennial
- ■ Zones 3–9
- ■ Attracts butterflies
- ■ Drought- and heat-tolerant

Elegant, ferny foliage and flat flower heads up to 3 inches wide make this all-purpose hardy perennial a garden favorite. Native to Europe, the Caucasus, and western Asia, it grows 1 to 3 feet tall.

USES: Yarrow adds substance to the middle of a border and color to the meadow garden. Attractive companions include ornamental grasses, lavenders, and Stokes' aster. Flower heads, composed of tightly packed, tiny flowers, last a long time when cut. You can also dry them for winter arrangements.

CULTURE: Yarrow, which resists both heat and drought, grows best in full sun in well-drained soil. In moist, fertile soil, it flops and may need staking. After a few years, yarrow forms a clump as wide as it is tall. Propagate by seed or division. Several species self-sow and can be invasive in the garden.

RECOMMENDED VARIETIES: 'Coronation Gold', 3 feet, bears golden blooms with gray-green leaves all summer. 'Moonshine' is similar with light yellow flowers from early summer to autumn. 'Fireland' has flowers that start brick red, then fade to pink and gold.

AGAPANTHUS SPP.

ag-a-PAN-this

Agapanthus

Agapanthus

- ■ Evergreen perennial
- ■ Zones 7–11
- ■ Long-lasting blue blooms
- ■ Shiny, straplike leaves
- ■ Good in containers

The evergreen leaves of this half-hardy perennial grow from a mass of hard, thick roots, making a clump from which arise bare stems topped with blue or white globes.

USES: In warm climates, agapanthus works well in borders, and its graceful habit and bright green leaves form a distinctive edging along paths. In colder climates, it performs well in pots; move them indoors over winter.

CULTURE: Agapanthus, a corm, likes full to partial sun and fertile, well-drained soil. Keep watered in spring, summer, and fall, but during dormancy let the corms dry out. Excellent in containers because it thrives when overcrowded. For best flowering, apply liquid fertilizer starting in early summer and ending when blooms form.

RECOMMENDED VARIETIES: 'Headbourne Hybrids', 15 to 36 inches tall, come in shades of blues and are among the most popular. 'Bressingham Blue' is a top-notch, deep blue cultivar 3 feet tall. 'Alba' is white, and 'Loch Hope' has dark violet, late-blooming flowers that reach 4 to 5 feet high.

AGASTACHE FOENICULUM

ag-a-STOCK-key fen-ICK-kew-lum

Anise hyssop

'Fragrant Delight' anise hyssop

- ■ Perennial
- ■ Zones 4–8
- ■ Attracts butterflies, bees, and hummingbirds
- ■ Edible leaves, flowers
- ■ Sweet, licorice scent

Each spring, one of the garden's prettiest sights is the emergence of anise hyssop as a clump of tender, purplish, heart-shaped leaves. By summer, this North American native stands 4 feet tall. Covered with 3-inch purple flower spikes, it creates an effective vertical accent.

USES: Anise hyssop makes a lovely addition to the herb garden or perennial border. Use flowers fresh or dried in arrangements. Add fresh leaves and flowers to salad or tea. Dried leaves and flowers make fragrant additions to potpourri.

CULTURE: Vigorous; best in full sun but will take a little shade. It likes average, moist but well-drained garden soil and may need staking if the soil is too fertile. A short-lived perennial, it self-sows abundantly. Excess plants are easy to transplant or pull from the garden.

RECOMMENDED VARIETIES: 'Tutti Frutti' has long-blooming pink blossoms on sturdy stems 2 feet high. 'Fragrant Delight' has light blue flower spikes. 'Fortune' is a superior new cultivar that grows 3 feet tall with dark blue flower spikes.

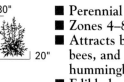

AGERATUM HOUSTONIANUM

a-jur-AY-tum hew-sto-nee-A-num

Flossflower

8"
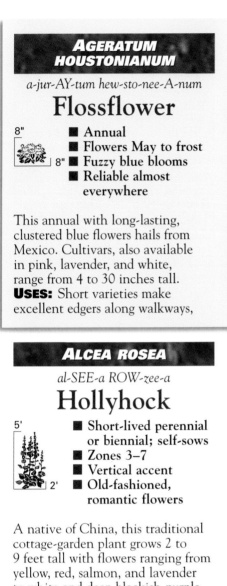
8"

- Annual
- Flowers May to frost
- Fuzzy blue blooms
- Reliable almost everywhere

This annual with long-lasting, clustered blue flowers hails from Mexico. Cultivars, also available in pink, lavender, and white, range from 4 to 30 inches tall.

USES: Short varieties make excellent edgers along walkways, at the front of the border, or bedded out in masses. Tall varieties work in the midborder and fill holes when early-blooming perennials are through producing flowers.

CULTURE: Flossflower grows in full sun to part shade in average garden soil. For maximum bloom, keep well watered and grow in fertile, well-drained soil. These are so easy to grow that you can sow seeds outdoors for late-season bloom or start them indoors to provide full-season flowers.

RECOMMENDED VARIETIES: 'Blue Horizon' grows up to 30 inches tall and is good for cutting. 'Blue Lagoon' is a bright blue bedder, reaching a uniform 8 inches in height. Early-blooming, 6-inch 'Summer Snow' has white flowers.

'Blue Horizon' flossflower

ALCEA ROSEA

al-SEE-a ROW-zee-a

Hollyhock

5'

2'

- Short-lived perennial or biennial; self-sows
- Zones 3–7
- Vertical accent
- Old-fashioned, romantic flowers

A native of China, this traditional cottage-garden plant grows 2 to 9 feet tall with flowers ranging from yellow, red, salmon, and lavender to white and deep blackish-purple. It combines well with old-fashioned flowers such as old garden roses, lavender, tree mallow, rose mallow, and Shasta daisies. The near-black flowers of 'Nigra' are outstanding with gloriosa daisies and sunflowers.

USES: Use at the back of the border and against fences and walls. Hollyhock foliage is prone to rust, a fungal disease, and Japanese beetles, so grow it with shorter plants in front to hide potential leaf damage.

CULTURE: Hollyhocks like well-drained, average garden soil in full sun. Pick off Japanese beetles by hand. To help avoid fungal diseases, grow plants far enough apart for adequate air circulation. Cut down and dispose of the debris at season's end. A biennial or short-lived perennial, hollyhocks self-sow freely.

RECOMMENDED VARIETIES: 'Chater's Double' has frilly double flowers; 'Indian Spring Hybrids' have single blooms; 'Nigra' has single, blackish-purple blooms.

'Indian Spring' hollyhock

AMARANTHUS CAUDATUS

am-a-RAN-thus caw-DAY-tus

Love-lies-bleeding

3'

2'

- Annual
- Droopy red tassels
- Tropical, exotic look
- Conversation piece
- Months of interest

Garden visitors gasp when they see the lax, sensuous, blood red tassels of love-lies-bleeding sag to the ground. This bizarre yet beautiful annual, a relic of grandmother's garden, stands 3 feet high and blooms all summer long.

USES: Grown in a mass, love-lies-bleeding adds an exotic note to the middle of the border. In an annual bed, it makes a dramatic backdrop for shorter flowers such as marigolds and compact zinnias. Love-lies-bleeding's floral tassels are long-lasting additions to fresh flower arrangements.

CULTURE: Prefers full sun and average, well-drained garden soil. Native to India and the Philippines, love-lies-bleeding tolerates dry soil and needs little watering once established.

RECOMMENDED VARIETIES: 'Viridis' reaches 3 to 4 feet high with bright chartreuse tassels. *A. tricolor* 'Joseph's Coat' is a tall, striking annual with brilliant large leaves in red, gold, and green. 'Illumination' grows 4 to 5 feet tall with scarlet, orange, and yellow leaves.

Love-lies-bleeding

AMSONIA HUBRECHTII

am-SOW-nee-uh hew-BREK-tee-eye

Arkansas amsonia

Blue star (Amsonia tabernaemontana)

30" | 20"

- Perennial
- Zones 3–9
- Clusters of steel blue, starlike flowers in spring
- Lacy, willowlike leaves turn brilliant yellow in fall
- Easy to grow

Resembling a 2-foot-tall willow tree, Arkansas amsonia is basically long-lived and maintenance free. It is one of the best perennials for reliable fall foliage color.

USES: Effective in masses, where the soft, willowlike texture contrasts with other garden plants. While it occasionally self-sows, this is a fuss-free plant that grows slowly and has few pests. It looks beautiful paired with Russian sage, asters, black-eyed Susan and ornamental grasses, and makes a lovely companion for peonies and poppies.

CULTURE: Plant in part shade or full sun in any soil, moist or dry. Set nursery plants 2 feet apart. Division is seldom necessary, and pests and diseases are not a problem. Seedlings are easy to pull up where they're not wanted. To keep plants short, shear back to 6 inches after flowering.

RECOMMENDED VARIETIES: Blue star (*A. tabernaemontana*) is very similar to Arkansas amsonia, with wider leaves, light blue flowers, and bright gold fall foliage.

ANTIRRHINUM MAJUS

an-tee-RYE-num MAY-jus

Snapdragon

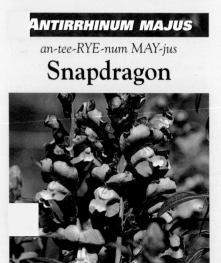

'Rocket Hybrid' snapdragon

18" | 10"

- Annual
- Heat-tolerant
- Good in bouquets
- Bright flowers from early summer to frost

Familiar yet diverse, snapdragons are a must for the easy flower garden. The flower spikes come in a rainbow of rich colors, from orange and lemon yellow to pink, lavender, white, bicolor, and a hummingbird-attracting red. These Mediterranean natives, ranging from 6 to 36 inches high, are tender perennials usually grown as annuals.

USES: Tall snaps work well toward the back of the border; medium varieties enhance the midborder; short varieties make excellent edging or bedding plants.

CULTURE: These easy flowers prefer well-drained soil in full sun to part shade. For bushy plants with lots of flowers, pinch off growing tips when the plants are young, and remove faded blooms. Benefits from monthly applications of fertilizer. Self-sows in good conditions.

RECOMMENDED VARIETIES: Heat-tolerant 'Rocket Hybrids' grow long spikes 30 to 36 inches tall. 'Madame Butterfly', 24 to 30 inches tall, has double blooms. 'Black Prince', 16 to 20 inches tall, has burgundy leaves and dark red blooms. 'Lipstick Silver', 18 inches tall, has white flowers with lavender tips.

AQUILEGIA SPP.

ak-wi-LEE-jah

Columbine

'Music Box' hybrid columbine

2' | 1'

- Perennial; some hybrids grown as annuals
- Zones 3–9
- Shade-loving
- Red, pink, blue, white, cream, yellow, and bicolor
- Attracts hummingbirds

These charming, late-spring plants sport odd-shaped flowers and decorative gray-green leaves.

USES: Tall specimens are perfect for woodland gardens and shady beds and borders; short ones work well in partly shaded rock gardens. Self-sowing makes columbine a good naturalized ground cover. Seedlings tend to hybridize or revert to a parent species.

CULTURE: Prefers dappled shade but also grows well in sun, especially in cooler climates. Columbine likes moist, well-drained soil high in organic matter. Renew leaves by cutting down after flowering.

RECOMMENDED VARIETIES: *A. vulgaris* 'Irish Elegance', 2 feet, has double ivory flowers flushed green at the tips; 'Nora Barlow' hybrids are double-flowered with pink-and-white, all-pink, or all-blue petals. *A. canadensis* is a 2- to 3-foot wildflower with early-blooming, dangling red-and-yellow flowers; *A. chrysantha* is similar with pale yellow flowers.

ASCLEPIAS TUBEROSA

a-SKLEE-pee-us too-ber-OH-suh

Butterfly weed

2'
2'

- Perennial
- Zones 3–9
- Orange flowers
- Attracts butterflies
- Drought-tolerant

This tough North American native comes from the prairie, where conditions may be hard, water scarce, and soils infertile. An excellent garden plant, it grows 2 to 3 feet tall.

USES: Good in meadows, borders, beach plantings, and butterfly gardens. Plant with ornamental grasses, coneflowers, and sage.

CULTURE: Heat-, salt-, and drought-tolerant, butterfly weed requires little care. Grow in full sun and average, well-drained soil. The taproot makes it hard to divide. Dig deep to lift the entire root mass when transplanting. Mark location in the garden; the new shoots don't appear until late spring.

RECOMMENDED VARIETIES: 'Gay Butterflies' has red, yellow, and orange flowers. *A. incarnata*, swamp milkweed, is 3 to 4 feet tall with pink flowers. It likes moist soil and attracts butterflies; its seedpods look good in dried arrangements. 'Cinderella', 3 to 4 feet tall, has pink and lavender flowers; 'Ice Ballet' has white flowers.

Butterfly weed

ASTER X FRIKARTII 'MONCH'

ASS-ter fri-KAR-tee-eye

Frikart's aster

3'
3'

- Perennial
- Zones 5–8
- Mass of blue daisies
- Blooms early summer to fall
- Attracts butterflies

This hybrid adds a soft blue color to the garden for an extraordinarily long season. It stands 2 to 3 feet tall and spreads up to 3 feet wide.

USES: Grow in meadow gardens or the fall border with boltonia, golden lace, black-eyed Susan, 'Autumn Joy' sedum, and miscanthus. Frikart's aster begins blooming earlier and lasts longer in the season than most asters, and has a more compact and dense habit. It makes an excellent cut flower.

CULTURE: Grow Frikart's aster in full sun in well-drained soil with good air circulation. Mulching helps it survive Zone 5 winters. Cut old plants to the ground in spring when new leaves have begun to emerge.

RECOMMENDED VARIETIES: 'Wonder of Staffa' has similar but flatter flowers. *A. novae-angliae* (New England aster, Zones 4–8) grows 4 to 6 feet tall and blooms late in the season; many cultivars are available. 'Purple Dome' is especially compact, forming a tight mound only 18 inches high covered in abundant deep purple flowers.

'Wonder of Staffa' Frickart's aster

ASTILBE SPP.

a-STILL-bee

Astilbe

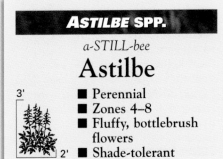

3'
2'

- Perennial
- Zones 4–8
- Fluffy, bottlebrush flowers
- Shade-tolerant

Plant early-, mid-, and late-season varieties and you can enjoy feathery astilbe nearly all summer. Varieties range from 1 to 4 feet high in pink, salmon, red, white, and rosy purple.

USES: Astilbe's colorful plumes create long-lasting vertical accents in shady beds and borders. It is also an effective ground cover, with green or bronzy fernlike leaves, and the plumes make good cut flowers. Bronze seed heads provide fall and winter interest.

CULTURE: Astilbe prefers moist, rich, humusy soil. Boost flower production with an application of fertilizer in spring. Cut back in fall or leave for winter interest.

RECOMMENDED VARIETIES: *A. × arendsii* 'Bressingham Beauty', 42 inches, has pink flowers in midsummer. 'Erica' and 'Rheinland' also have pink plumes in midseason but grow only 20 inches high. Early-summer white 'Deutschland' is 2 feet high. 'White Gloria' is similar but blooms in late summer. *A. chinensis* 'Pumila', an 8- to 12-inch ground cover, has pink flowers in late summer and tolerates dry soil. 'Finale' is another late-summer pink, 18 inches tall. 'Superba' has reddish-purple flowers in late season and reaches 30 to 40 inches high.

'Erica' astilbe

BEGONIA X SEMPERFLORENS-CULTORUM

beh-GO-nee-ah sem-per-FLO-rens-kul-TOR-rum

Wax begonia

'Cocktail Brandy' wax begonia

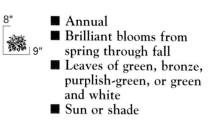

8"
9"

- Annual
- Brilliant blooms from spring through fall
- Leaves of green, bronze, purplish-green, or green and white
- Sun or shade

Wax begonias brighten dark corners with colorful leaves and waxy red, pink, or white flowers. Native to Brazil, they are tender perennials grown as annuals.

USES: Shady places benefit from wax begonias' colorful presence and branching, bushy habit. They look good edging paths, massed in beds, and at the front of the border. They are also terrific in containers.

CULTURE: Wax begonias prefer shade, though they can survive in sun when watered well or where summers are cool. They thrive in rich, moist, well-drained soil.

RECOMMENDED VARIETIES: 'Lotto Hybrids' have 2½-inch pink or red flowers. 'Party Red Bronze' has dark bronze leaves and scarlet flowers on 12-inch plants. 'Paint Splash' has white-variegated leaves. The 'Cocktail' series has bronze leaves. *B. × tuberhybrida*, tuberous begonia, has huge single or double flowers up to 5 inches wide in red, pink, orange, yellow, and white. Trailing varieties are good in hanging baskets. The 'Nonstop' series is excellent for bedding.

BOLTONIA ASTEROIDES

bowl-TOE-nee-ah as-te-ROY-deez

Boltonia

'Snowbank' boltonia

5'
3'

- Perennial
- Zones 4–9
- Fall flowering
- Asterlike blooms
- Available in pink or white
- Vertical accent
- Tolerates heat and humidity

Easy-to-grow boltonia adds life and color to the autumn garden. At 3 to 6 feet tall, it provides much-needed vertical interest.

USES: Grow in meadows, at the back of the border, or against fences and walls where you can appreciate its imposing height. This is a good cut flower for fall arrangements.

CULTURE: Boltonia, native to the central United States, does best in full sun and average, well-drained soil but can grow in light shade and poor soil. Plants grown in these conditions will be shorter. It tolerates heat, humidity, and drought. Plants may need staking to keep them upright in wind, rain, shady spots, or rich soil. Cut plants back by half in early June for a more compact habit. Prune back by one-third in mid-July for later flowering and shorter plants. Increase by division or cuttings in spring.

RECOMMENDED VARIETIES: 'Snowbank' has white flowers on a 4-foot plant. 'Pink Beauty' has pink flowers and a more relaxed habit.

BUDDLEIA DAVIDII

BUD-lee-ah da-VI-dee-eye

Butterfly bush

'Black Knight' butterfly bush

10'
6'

- Shrub
- Zones 5–9
- Attracts butterflies
- Graceful, fragrant flower spikes

This arching, tender shrub, 5 to 15 feet high, bears flower spikes in shades of white, lavender, blue, pink, purple, and yellow. It starts blooming in mid- to late summer and continues into fall, depending on its location. Native to China.

USES: Use butterfly bush in mixed borders, in butterfly gardens, and massed. The tapering, scented flower spikes are good in arrangements.

CULTURE: Butterfly bush grows best in full sun in fertile, moist, well-drained soil. In ideal conditions, it self-sows freely, creating volunteers that are easily transplanted or pulled from the garden. In cold-winter areas, its top growth dies to the ground in winter. Cutting the plant to the ground in early spring renews it and keeps its height at 5 to 10 feet.

RECOMMENDED VARIETIES: 'Black Knight', 8 to 10 feet, has dark purple flowers up to 8 inches long. 'Lochinch' has lavender flowers with orange eyes. Butterflies particularly adore the 12-inch pink flower spikes of 'Pink Delight'. 'White Profusion' is a good white cultivar. *B. alternifolia* has purple flowers on a plant up to 20 feet tall.

CALENDULA OFFICINALIS

ka-LEN-dew-lah oh-fi-shi-NAL-iss

Pot marigold

20" 12"

- Annual
- Bright yellow or orange ray flowers
- Attractive addition to garden salads
- Flowers for months

This fuss-free Mediterranean native is a favorite cottage-garden plant from 8 inches to 2 feet tall. It lights up the flower garden with cheerful blooms in hot summer colors.
USES: Use pot marigold in herb, medicinal, or grandmother gardens.

Grow it in pots, massed in beds, at the front of the border with other hot-colored flowers, or with flowers of contrasting color such as dwarf morning glory. Add chopped rays of flowers grown without chemicals to salads for a colorful garnish.
CULTURE: Grows best in full sun and well-drained, moist soil. It will stop blooming during the high heat of summer, but will continue in fall.
RECOMMENDED VARIETIES: 'Bon Bon Hybrids' have 3-inch flowers in yellow, apricot, or orange. 'Calypso Hybrids' have 4-inch orange or yellow daisylike blooms with brown centers on 8-inch plants. 'Prince Mix' has double, 3-inch flowers on heat-tolerant,

2½-foot plants. 'Déjà Vu' is 21 inches tall, a mixture of pink, orange, yellow, and cream with burnt orange; some blossoms have darker tips. 'Red Splash' is a mix for borders and cutting.

'Bon Bon Orange' pot marigold

CANNA HYBRIDS

KAN-a

Canna

6' 2'

- Perennial often grown as an annual
- Zones 7–11
- Large flowers
- Big tropical leaves

Canna's striking leaves grow up to 2 feet long and 6 inches wide in shades of green, blue-green, purple, and bronze. Plants can reach 2 to 8 feet tall topped with flowers in red, pink, orange, or yellow.
USES: Cannas add height and formality to garden beds. Tall

varieties work well in the back of the border, and all sizes make excellent container plants.
CULTURE: Grow in sun and well-drained soil. Canna thrives in fertile soil with plenty of water and organic matter. To overwinter, dig, wash, and dry rhizomes in fall and store over winter in spaghnum or vermiculite in a cool, dry place. Replant in potting soil in early spring, and plant outdoors after frost danger has passed.
RECOMMENDED VARIETIES: 'Red King Humbert' is 6 to 8 feet tall with dark bronze leaves and scarlet flowers. 'Black Knight' is similar but lower growing to about 4 feet, with dark red flowers.

'Praetoria' (also called 'Bengal Tiger') reaches 6 feet tall with dazzling yellow-striped leaves and orange flowers. 'Picasso' is a 3-foot dwarf with yellow flowers speckled with red. 'Pink Futurity' has pink flowers and burgundy leaves.

'Red King Humbert' canna

CAPSICUM ANNUUM

KAP-si-kum AN-you-um

Ornamental pepper

15" 12"

- Annual
- Brilliant fruit
- Tolerates heat and humidity
- Late-season interest

Native to the American tropics, ornamental peppers bear bright red, purple, orange, yellow, or creamy white fruit on plants 10 to 20 inches high. The edible fruit is fiery hot.

USES: Makes a compact edger, a good filler for the hot-colored garden, and a decorative addition to the kitchen garden. Also excels in indoor and outdoor containers and in plantings with marigolds, moss rose, and cockscomb.
CULTURE: Grow in full sun to light shade in well-drained, average garden soil. You can increase the plant's ability to fruit by supplying plenty of water and organic matter.
RECOMMENDED VARIETIES: 'Black Prince' has black leaves and fruits that turn from black to red. 'Holiday Cheer' is compact with round fruit that goes from cream to purple-tinged yellow to red. 'Pretty in Purple' has dark purple and

greenish leaves and round fruit less than 1 inch in diameter. Fruit starts out purple and changes to yellow, orange, and scarlet.

'Treasure Red' ornamental pepper

CATHARANTHUS ROSEUS

ka-the-RAN-thus ROW-zee-us

Vinca

'Cooler Raspberry Red' vinca

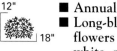

12"
18"

- Annual
- Long-blooming flowers in shades of white, pink, or red
- Tolerates heat, drought, and air pollution

Vinca blooms nonstop from early summer to frost. It grows into a 6- to 16-inch spreading mound with flowers 2 inches wide in shades of pink, white, red, lavender, and apricot, often with contrasting eye. Native to Madagascar and India.
USES: Works well in beds, borders, containers, and hanging baskets. Use for an annual ground cover, or grow indoors in winter.

CULTURE: Best in full sun. Spreads 18 to 24 inches; for a ground cover effect, set plants 12 inches apart in well-drained, humusy garden soil. For best results, water regularly and fertilize lightly. Vinca is heat- and drought-tolerant, but suffers in moist, cool-summer climates.
RECOMMENDED VARIETIES: 'Stardust Orchid' is bright orchid with a star-shaped, central white eye. 'Parasol' has abundant 2-inch white flowers with a rosy eye. 'Pretty in Rose' has dark pink, phloxlike flowers. 'Cooler' series has 2½-inch flowers in icy pink, light pink with a deep pink eye, rose, raspberry, and peppermint; it grows up to 14 inches tall.

CELOSIA ARGENTEA VAR. CRISTATA

sell-OH-zee-uh ar-JEN-tee-uh kris-TAH-tuh

Cockscomb

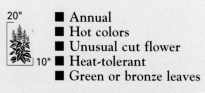

20"
10"

- Annual
- Hot colors
- Unusual cut flower
- Heat-tolerant
- Green or bronze leaves

Cockscomb's dense, wavy crests are eye-catching. Flower heads in shades of red, yellow, and orange measure up to 10 inches across. Plants grow 4 to 40 inches high.
USES: Use in beds, borders, and pots. Grow massed or as a specimen. Crested cockscomb also makes a good cut flower, fresh or dried.
CULTURE: Grow cockscomb in full sun in moist but well-drained, humusy soil. It tolerates lean soil but performs better with regular

'Century Yellow' cockscomb

watering and light fertilization. Sow seeds indoors 6 to 8 weeks before date of last frost. Sprinkle seeds with a thin layer of seed-starting mix and keep moist.
RECOMMENDED VARIETIES: 'Chief Hybrids' have strong, single stems up to 40 inches high with red, rose, yellow, or orange plumes, excellent for cutting. The 'Century' series is one of the best bedders, 20 to 30 inches high. 'New Look' has glowing red plumes and dark purple foliage on 20-inch plants. C. *argentea* var. *spicata*, wheat celosia, has small flower spikes on tall, sturdy stems, suitable for cutting or informal bedding. 'Pink Candle' has rose-pink plumes on 30-inch stems.

CERATOSTIGMA PLUMBAGINOIDES

sa-rat-oh-STIG-muh plum-ba-jih-NOY-deez

Blue plumbago

Blue plumbago

10"
15"

- Perennial
- Zones 5–9
- Intense blue flowers
- Vigorous ground cover
- Reddish-bronze fall color

The golden, slanting light of late summer enhances the deep blue blossoms of this 10- to 12-inch perennial, which spreads 12 to 18 inches wide. Native to China.
USES: This low-growing plant looks handsome in rock gardens and under trees, where its spreading habit makes it a superb ground cover. It is perfect to cover the yellowing foliage of early spring-blooming bulbs such

as crocus and grape hyacinth, and is lovely with fall-blooming crocus (Colchicum spp.).
CULTURE: Blue plumbago likes well-drained soil in sun to partial shade. Leave old stems until spring; sprouts emerge late. Then cut back dead matter so it will not crowd new growth. Divide plants in spring if the center dies out. Mulch lightly in Zone 5 for winter protection.
RECOMMENDED VARIETIES: C. *willmottianum*, Chinese leadwort, is a deciduous shrub hardy to Zone 8 with hairy leaf margins and more drought tolerance than C. *plumbaginoides*. 'Forest Blue' has blue flowers and an erect habit 2 feet tall; it is hardy to Zone 7.

CHRYSANTHEMUM X LEUCANTHEMUM

krih-SAN-thu-mum loo-KAN-thu-mum

Shasta daisy

2'

- Perennial
- Zones 5–9
- Pure white daisies with yellow centers
- Blooms early summer

2'

Shasta daisy is available with single or frilly double flowers 3 to 5 inches wide. It grows 1 to 3 feet tall.

USES: This familiar garden plant helps unify the pink, blue, and lemon yellow flowers of the early-summer border. It also works well in meadow gardens. Its long, sturdy stems make it excellent for cutting. Dwarf cultivars such as 'Snow Lady' (10 to 12 inches) or 'Little Miss Muffet' (8 to 12 inches) are charming rock garden plants.

CULTURE: This is a short-lived perennial that likes moist, well-drained soil in full sun to partial shade. Good winter drainage is crucial. Pinch growing tips in spring to keep tall types lush. Selected cultivars behave better than the species, which tends to spread by seed and by root.

RECOMMENDED VARIETIES: 'Becky' is the longest blooming, with single flowers over 6 to 8 weeks on 30-inch plants. It is also the most heat-tolerant. 'Alaska' is a 3-foot plant with 3- to 5-inch single flowers, hardy to Zone 3. 'Aglaia' produces double 3-inch blossoms but is not as vigorous as the species. 'Little Princess' is a 12-inch dwarf.

'Aglaia' Shasta daisy

CISTUS SPP.

SIS-tuss

Rock rose

3'

- Evergreen shrub
- Zones 8–10
- Poppylike blooms in early spring
- Evergreen leaves
- Good seaside shrub

5'

This short-lived Mediterranean shrub has flowers in pink, rosy red, purple, and white, usually with a contrasting center. Most selections measure 3 to 4 feet high, but heights can range from 1 to 7 feet.

USES: Drought-tolerant and salt-tolerant, this low-growing shrub works well as an oceanside ground cover or a bank planting on the West Coast. It has an irregular, mounded habit.

CULTURE: Rock rose thrives in full sun and fast-draining soil. Pinching growing tips of new plants encourages fullness. Avoid hard pruning, and don't transplant once it is established.

RECOMMENDED VARIETIES: 'Silver Pink' is 2 feet tall with gray-green foliage, bright yellow stamen clusters, and pink petals that are pale at the base. 'Peggy Sammons' produces delicate pink flowers on a 4-foot plant with gray-green leaves and downy stems. *C. laurifolius* is the hardiest species, growing up to 6 feet tall with 2- to 3-inch yellow-centered white blossoms and leathery leaves. *C. salviifolius* (sageleaf rock rose) has white flowers in spring on 3-foot, gray-leaved plants.

White rock rose (Cistus × hybridus)

CLEMATIS SPP.

KLEM-ah-tiss

Clematis

10'

- Perennial vines
- Zones 3–9
- Lavish flowers
- Climbing, shrubby, and draping forms

4'

This dazzling plant can produce spring-to-fall interest in the garden. Small-flowered species bloom mid- to late spring. Large-flowered hybrids bloom early to midsummer or mid- to late summer. Flower colors range from white to pink, yellow, purple, violet, and bicolored.

USES: Clematis climbs up and through supports, clinging by twining stems and leaves. Grow on arbors, trellises, pergolas, roses, and telephone poles with netting attached.

CULTURE: Clematis needs moist, cool soil and excellent drainage. It likes sun aboveground and the coolness of shade for its roots. When planting, bury the stems 2 to 3 inches deep so the plant sends out new shoots. A layer of mulch cools roots and helps retain soil moisture. Prune most clematis shortly after flowering. Some varieties die to the ground in winter. Remove dead stems in early spring right after new shoots appear.

RECOMMENDED VARIETIES: It's hard to go wrong with any large-flowered hybrid. Jackman clematis blooms longest, with violet-purple flowers from early to late summer.

'Ramona' hybrid clematis

CLEOME HASSLERIANA

klee-OH-mee hass-luh-RAH-nah

Spider flower

'Violet Queen' spider flower

■ Annual
■ Long-blooming, airy flowers
■ Seedpods like spider legs
■ Drought-tolerant
■ Reliable self-sower

This South American native blooms nonstop from May or June to frost. Flowers can be white or purple, and leaves look like pointed fingers on a hand.

USES: Spider flower suits Victorian bedding plans. It looks stunning planted in a mass behind Chinese asters and dusty miller. Plant it at the back of the border or against a fence. Because of its airy stature, you can also use it in the midborder as a see-through plant, an especially lovely effect against large, bold cannas. Although spider flower is short-lived when cut, it is lovely in old-fashioned bouquets.

CULTURE: Spider flower thrives in full sun to partial shade, moist garden soil, and heat. The spiny plant self-sows freely, but unwanted volunteers are easy to pull out.

RECOMMENDED VARIETIES: The 'Queen' series produces plants 4 feet tall with white, pink, violet, or rose flowers. 'Violet Queen' is a particularly handsome plant with deep violet blooms. 'White Queen' is a soft, muted white. 'Cherry Queen' is bright cherry rose.

CLETHRA ALNIFOLIA

KLE-thra all-ni-FOH-lee-uh

Summersweet

Summersweet

■ Deciduous shrub
■ Zones 3–9
■ White bottlebrush flowers in late summer
■ Honey fragrance
■ Yellow fall color

A native of eastern North America, summersweet grows 8 feet tall and wide with scented pink or white bottlebrush flowers in late summer and bright yellow fall foliage.

USES: This shrub works well throughout the garden but especially in wet, shady spots. It's a lovely addition to woodland gardens and mixed borders and a good companion for Joe-Pye weed, spiderwort, and rose mallow.

CULTURE: Grow summersweet in moist, acid soil rich with organic matter. Plant the shrub in early spring and keep well-watered. Raise the planting several inches higher than the soil level and mulch it so the mulch doesn't touch the stems. Summersweet will keep its natural oval shape if pruned after blooming in late summer.

RECOMMENDED VARIETIES: 'Hummingbird', a spreading, mounded dwarf, is an attractive ground cover shrub 2 to 3 feet high and wide. 'Paniculata' has plentiful, long flower spikes. 'Ruby Spice' has rosy flowers with persistent color. 'Rosea' has pinkish-white flowers.

CONSOLIDA AMBIGUA

kon-SAH-li-dah am-BIG-you-ah

Larkspur

'Early Bird Hybrids' larkspur

■ Annual
■ Tall flower spikes
■ Good cut flower
■ Cottage-garden plant
■ Self-sowing

The pink, purple, violet-blue, rose, and white blooms of annual larkspur resemble perennial delphiniums in shape. Native to southern Europe, larkspur grows 1 to 2 feet tall and blooms through fall where summers are cool.

USES: Larkspur is perfect for cottage gardens, meadow gardens, or in the middle of the border. It makes an excellent cut flower.

CULTURE: Grow larkspur in rich, moist garden soil in full sun to light shade. If desired, you can prevent self-sowing tendencies by deadheading fading flowers before they set seed. Some varieties of this upright-branching annual grow 4 to 5 feet tall and may need staking. In hot climates, larkspur will stop blooming in the intense heat of midsummer. To propagate, sow seeds straight into the garden in late autumn or early spring.

RECOMMENDED VARIETIES: 'Early Bird Hybrids' are 20 inches tall and bloom early in the season. 'Giant Imperial Hybrids' grow 2 to 3 feet tall with double flowers in pink, blue, and white. The 'Dwarf Hyacinth' series has spikes of tubular flowers on 1-foot-high plants.

CONVOLVULUS TRICOLOR

kon-VOL-vew-lus TRY-kuh-lor

Dwarf morning glory

12"
15"
- ■ Annual
- ■ Flowers open by day
- ■ Blooms all summer
- ■ Neat, mounded form

Dwarf morning glory grows into a bushy mound 1 foot high and up to 1½ feet wide. Flared, 2-inch flowers have a white band separating a yellow throat from a deep blue margin. Also available in white, pink, rose, and lavender.

USES: Dwarf morning glory works well in beds and containers. It makes a colorful edging and an eye-catching rock garden plant. Grow with 'Early Sunrise' coreopsis, signet marigold, or 'Friendly Yellow' annual statice.

CULTURE: Grow in full sun in average, well-drained garden soil. Dwarf morning glory tolerates heat and poor soil. For best flowering, do not fertilize.

RECOMMENDED VARIETIES: The 'Ensign' series comes with royal blue, light blue, white, or rose margins. *C. sabatius*, ground morning glory, is an evergreen perennial hardy in Zones 8–10 and excellent for dry, lean soil. It grows

1 to 2 feet high, spreads to 3 feet or more, and is covered in light blue flowers from early summer to early winter.

'Royal Ensign' dwarf morning glory

COREOPSIS SPP.

koh-ree-OP-sis

Coreopsis

2'
2'
- ■ Perennial
- ■ Zones 5–9
- ■ Yellow daisylike flowers
- ■ Summer-long bloom
- ■ Drought-tolerant

This versatile perennial grows 6 to 36 inches tall and is native to the United States, tropical Africa, or the Hawaiian Islands, depending on the species. Daisylike flowers come in shades of yellow or pink. Some self-sow; others spread by roots.

USES: Grow coreopsis in perennial borders, meadow gardens, and wildflower gardens. It also works well in containers and on slopes.

CULTURE: Plant in full sun in average, well-drained garden soil. Plants tolerate heat and dry soil and flop when grown in rich, moist conditions. After the first flush of bloom, cut plants back to stimulate fall flowering.

RECOMMENDED VARIETIES: *C. verticillata* 'Moonbeam' has delicate, threadlike leaves and pale yellow flowers on an 18- to 24-inch-plant. *C. rosea* 'American Dream' bears pink flowers on a 1-foot plant. *C. grandiflora* 'Early Sunrise' has 2-inch semidouble golden flowers

on an 18-inch plant. *C. auriculata* 'Nana' grows 6 to 9 inches tall and bears yellow blooms in late spring.

'Moonbeam' threadleaf coreopsis

CORYDALIS LUTEA

koh-RID-ah-lis loo-TEE-ah

Yellow corydalis

12"
18"
- ■ Perennial
- ■ Zones 5–7
- ■ Pale yellow snapdragonlike blooms
- ■ Delicate blue-green leaves

Corydalis, an English cottage-garden classic, forms a low (12- to 15-inch) mound that self-sows in shady spots. Like Japanese bleeding heart, it fades away in heat and humidity, but in cooler climates it

blooms from spring to fall. Native to southeastern Europe.

USES: Yellow corydalis adds charm to nooks in stone walls and between flagstone pavers. It's also a good edging for shady perennial borders. Grow with columbine, fringed bleeding heart, and coral bells.

CULTURE: Grow yellow corydalis in partial shade in moist, rich, well-drained soil. Deadheading promotes rebloom. Because yellow corydalis is hard to divide or transplant, it's better to establish new, young plants in the garden. Once established, it self-sows freely and naturalizes in optimal conditions.

RECOMMENDED VARIETIES: *C. flexuosa* 'Blue Panda' has

delightful blue flowers on a 12- to 15-inch mound of leaves. *C. ochroleuca* produces creamy white flowers and blue-gray leaves.

Yellow corydalis

COSMOS SPP.

KOZ-mohs

Cosmos

'Sonata' cosmos

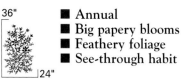

36"
24"

- Annual
- Big papery blooms
- Feathery foliage
- See-through habit

Cosmos lends a light touch to the garden with its fine-textured foliage and thin-petaled, pastel flowers. *C. bipinnatus* comes in shades of pink, rose, crimson, and white, *C. sulphureus* in shades of orange and yellow. Both bloom from June to frost. Cosmos has a bushy habit, growing 3 to 4 feet tall with flowers 4 to 6 inches wide. Good companions are 'Lulu' signet marigold, creamy white zinnias, and 'Fiesta del Sol' Mexican sunflower.

USES: Grow cosmos at the back of the border or weaving through flower beds for a more casual look.
CULTURE: Easy to grow from seed directly sown in the garden. Best in full sun and well-drained, lean to average soil; fertile soil promotes more leaves than blooms. Pinch back growing tips for a bushier plant. Cosmos frequently self-sows.
RECOMMENDED VARIETIES: 'Sonata Hybrids' series has 3- to 4-inch flowers in white, pink, rose, and crimson on 3½-foot plants. The *C. sulphureus* 'Cosmic' series is good for beds, pots, and cutting, with 2-inch orange or yellow, double or semidouble flowers on 1- to 2-foot, heat- and drought-resistant plants.

COTINUS COGGYGRIA

ko-TYE-nus ko-GIG-ree-a

Smokebush

'Royal Purple' smokebush

15'
15'

- Deciduous tree or large shrub
- Zones 5–8
- Clouds of flowers
- Green or purple foliage

Huge panicles of smoky pink to mauve are evident on this plant from June to September. Native from southern Europe to central China, this shrub has an open, rounded habit and rounded, smooth-edged, green or purple leaves. It grows up to 15 feet tall and 15 feet wide.

USES: Smokebush makes an exotic addition to shrub and mixed borders, and a wonderful backdrop for the perennial bed. It looks good with black-eyed Susan and purple coneflower, or as a support for pink, purple, or white clematis.
CULTURE: Smokebush thrives in full sun and adapts to a variety of soils, including dry, rocky ones. It is drought-tolerant once established but needs deep, thorough watering when young. Prune to remove dead branches.
RECOMMENDED VARIETIES: 'Royal Purple' and 'Velvet Cloak' have nonfading, deep purple leaves with purplish-red flower heads and intense reddish-purple fall color. 'Day Dream' has green leaves; persistent, lavish, mauve-pink blooms; and a thicker habit.

DIANTHUS BARBATUS

dye-AN-thus bar-BAY-tus

Sweet William

'Rondo' sweet William

8"
6"

- Biennial in Zones 3–8, but often grown as an annual
- Old-fashioned, clustered flower heads
- Red, pink, purple, or white blooms
- Good for cutting

This cottage-garden favorite bears long-lasting flowers in blends of mostly red, pink, purple, and white. Sweet William grows 4 to 18 inches high. Old varieties may be fragrant; newer ones are bred more for size and color.

USES: Grow in rock gardens, cottage gardens, flower beds, crevices in rock walls, and at the front of the border. Strong stems and long-lasting blooms make it a good cut flower. Grow with sweet alyssum and petunias.
CULTURE: Prefers moist, limy, well-drained soil in full sun to partial shade. It blooms from late spring to early summer and may rebloom later in the season if trimmed back after flowering. A biennial, it self-sows.
RECOMMENDED VARIETIES: 'Double Dwarf Midget' has mostly double flowers in pink, red, and white. 'Harlequin' has pink and white spherical flower heads. 'Dunnets Dark Crimson', 18 inches high, has deep red flowers and reddish-purple leaves.

DIANTHUS DELTOIDES

dye-AN-thus del-TOY-deez

Maiden pink

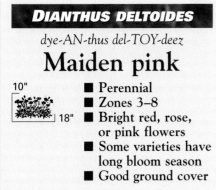

10" 18"

- Perennial
- Zones 3–8
- Bright red, rose, or pink flowers
- Some varieties have long bloom season
- Good ground cover

Maiden pink produces dainty, five-petaled blossoms with green or gray leaves. It measures 6 to 12 inches tall and spreads 12 to 20 inches wide.

USES: Its vigor and spreading, trailing habit make it an excellent ground cover. It also looks good in rock gardens and cottage gardens, in wall cracks, or spilling over the top of a retaining wall. Good companions are lavender, thyme, germander, and old garden roses.

CULTURE: Grow this self-sowing perennial in well-drained soil in full sun. It prefers alkaline conditions, but will bloom in slightly acid soil. Shear after flowering in early summer for fall rebloom. Pinks prefer cool summers; in the South, grow heat-tolerant varieties.

RECOMMENDED VARIETIES: 'Zing Rose' and 'Zing Salmon' produce thick evergreen mats 6 inches high. They bloom from spring to fall, and self-sow. *D. gratianopolitanus* 'Bath's Pink' has a spicy fragrance, pink blossoms, and blue-green leaves. Blooming for about a month in early summer, it is more heat-resistant than *D. deltoides* and a good choice for the South.

'Bath's Pink' dianthus

DICENTRA EXIMIA

dye-SEN-truh ek-ZIM-ee-uh

Fringed bleeding heart

30" 18"

- Perennial
- Zones 3–9
- Pink flowers from spring to frost
- Shade-loving ground cover
- Fine-textured foliage

This attractive perennial, native to woodlands in the eastern United States, spreads quickly by seed to produce 18- to 24-inch clumps of ferny, blue-green leaves and delicate, deep pink flowers.

USES: Use as a ground cover in shady gardens. Plant in beds around trees and shrubs or along walls.

CULTURE: Likes partial shade and moist, well-drained soil rich in organic matter. Self-sows freely.

RECOMMENDED VARIETIES: 'Luxuriant' produces abundant cerise blooms all summer and grows 12 to 18 inches tall. 'Snowdrift' and 'Snowflakes' are similar, in white. *D. formosa* 'Zestful' is spring-flowering in deep rose. *D. spectabilis,* Japanese bleeding heart, is hardy in Zones 2–8. It has exotic dark pink, heart-shaped flowers in May and June on an open-branching plant 3 feet tall and wide. Cut it to the ground when it starts going dormant after flowering. 'Alba' has pure white flowers.

Fringed bleeding heart

DIGITALIS PURPUREA

dih-gi-TAL-iss pur-PUR-ee-uh

Foxglove

4' 3'

- Biennial
- Zones 4–8
- Spikes of nodding, tubular flowers
- Traditional cottage-garden plant

This charming biennial blooms with the old roses in early summer. Height ranges from 2 to 5 feet tall.

USES: Foxglove adds vertical interest to any landscape. It is perfect for the middle of the informal border, against walls and fences, and in cottage and woodland gardens, where it naturalizes.

CULTURE: Foxglove thrives in part shade and moist, well-drained, acid soil rich in organic matter, although in cool climates it tolerates more sun. It is a constant presence in the garden because of its tendency to self-sow; seedlings form basal leaves the first year and bloom the second.

RECOMMENDED VARIETIES: 'Alba' is a pure white form. 'Foxy', 3 feet, produces rose, yellow, and white flowers. 'Excelsior Hybrids' grow 5 feet tall with pink, rose, mauve, white, and yellow flower spikes. 'Giant Shirley' has 3-foot flower spikes in white to shell pink and dark pink on a plant up to 5 feet tall. *D. × mertonensis* is a hardy perennial 3 to 4 feet tall with strawberry pink flower spikes.

'Giant Shirley' foxglove

DOLICHOS LABLAB (LABLAB PURPUREUS)

DOH-li-kohs LAB-lab

Hyacinth bean

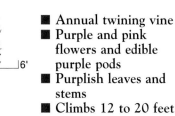

- Annual twining vine
- Purple and pink flowers and edible purple pods
- Purplish leaves and stems
- Climbs 12 to 20 feet in a summer

Hyacinth bean

With its colorful flowers, fruit, and foliage, hyacinth bean stays attractive from summer to frost. Native to tropical Africa, this tender perennial is hardy in Zones 9–10, but it's grown as an annual in most of the United States. **USES:** Decorate walls, fences, and trellises with this vine. Let it scramble over nearby plants, weaving its way through the mixed border. Contrasting companions include gold and orange varieties of Mexican sunflower and sunflowers. **CULTURE:** Plant hyacinth bean in late spring in well-drained garden soil of average fertility. Rich, fertile soil encourages an abundance of leaves but discourages ample flowering. This plant likes a warm, sunny location. Seeds are easy to harvest from dried pods. **RECOMMENDED VARIETIES:** 'Ruby Moon' has bicolored pink blossoms and dark brownish-purple pods. 'Alba' produces white to pale lavender flowers with green pods and foliage.

ECHINACEA PURPUREA

eh-ki-NAY-see-a pur-PUR-ee-a

Purple coneflower

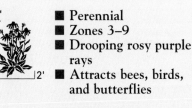

- Perennial
- Zones 3–9
- Drooping rosy purple rays
- Attracts bees, birds, and butterflies

'Magnus' purple coneflower

This wildflower, native to the North American prairie, attracts attention for its striking blooms from summer to fall. It ranges from 2 to 4 feet tall and produces flowers from 4 to 6 inches wide. **USES:** Purple coneflower belongs in beds and borders and makes an ideal addition to meadow gardens. Sturdy stems and an attractive form make it good for cutting. Minus the rays, which are short-lived when cut, the long-lasting central cone is a welcome addition to both fresh and dried arrangements. **CULTURE:** This tough landscape plant needs little attention once established. It prefers full sun and well-drained, average garden soil. Purple coneflower is both drought- and heat-tolerant. When grown in too much shade or too-rich soil, it may flop and need staking. **RECOMMENDED VARIETIES:** 'Bravado', 4 feet high, has 6-inch flowers with wide, horizontal petals. 'Magnus', a vivid purplish-red, also has horizontal rays. 'White Swan', 2 to 3 feet tall, has pure white rays. 'Bright Star' has rosy pink rays and bronze cones.

ERIGERON SPP.

uh-RIH-ja-ron

Fleabane

- Perennial
- Zones 4–9 (Zone 7 east of the Rockies)
- Blue or pink daisies
- Good for cutting

'Pink Jewel' fleabane

Native to western North America, fleabane blooms from early summer into fall. Hybrids have flowers ranging from ½ inch to 1 inch wide in shades of violet-blue, pink, white, red, and lavender on a 1- to 2-foot plant with a similar spread. **USES:** Grow on retaining walls or in rock gardens, rock walls, and sunny beds and borders. Small cultivars work well in paving cracks, window boxes, and hanging baskets. Use larger hybrids for cutting. Planted in groups of three or more, fleabane works well with blue flowers such as 'Victoria' salvia and 'Oxford Blue' love-in-a-mist. **CULTURE:** Plant about a foot apart in full sun and very well-drained, sandy, light soil. Cut back after blooming to refresh foliage. Stake tall varieties where necessary. *E. karvinskianus* readily self-sows. **RECOMMENDED VARIETIES:** 'Adria', 2 feet high, has big lavender-blue flowers. 'Pink Jewel', 30 inches, has bright pink, semidouble flowers. *E. karvinskianus* (Mexican daisy, Zones 8–10) produces ½-inch pink and white blooms all summer on a 10- to 20-inch plant. 'Moerheimeri' is a lavender form.

ESCHSCHOLZIA CALIFORNICA

eh-SHOAL-tsee-a ca-li-FOR-ni-ka

California poppy

12"
15"

- Annual
- Bright orange, red, pink, yellow, or creamy white flowers
- Fine-textured gray-green leaves
- Drought-tolerant

This sturdy West Coast native grows 1 foot tall and spreads somewhat wider, forming a gray-green mound topped by brilliant orange flowers in the landscape. Cultivars are available in a wide range of warm colors.

USES: Creates a stunning display massed on sunny slopes and hillsides; it's also good in beds, borders, and rock gardens.

CULTURE: Grow in lean, sandy, alkaline, well-drained soil. Prefers full sun but tolerates some shade. Do not fertilize or overwater. Best grown from seed sown directly in the garden after the last frost in cool climates. In warm areas, broadcast the seed outdoors in fall and winter. Self-sows once established.

RECOMMENDED VARIETIES: The 'Thai Silk' series, 10 inches, produces semidouble, papery, cup-shaped flowers from spring to midsummer in a range of hot pastels. 'Thai Silk Appleblossom' is a delicate pink-and-white bicolor. 'Aurantiaca' has bright orange flowers and threadlike leaves.

'Monarch Mixed' California poppy

EUPATORIUM PURPUREUM

you-pah-TOR-ee-um pur-PUR-ee-um

Joe-Pye weed

6'
3'

- Perennial
- Zones 3–8
- Big rosy purple blooms
- Moisture-loving
- Attracts butterflies

This giant wildflower is native to eastern North America. It grows 6 to 8 feet tall with purplish flower heads up to 1 foot across.

USES: Because of its mass, Joe-Pye weed gives architectural interest to a garden and works well at the back of the border or the center of an island planting. Its imposing presence is dramatic in meadow gardens, cottage gardens, and naturalized in damp, low-lying areas.

CULTURE: Grow in moist soil in sun to partial shade. Mildew can be disfiguring; thin for better air circulation. Divide clumps in spring when necessary. This is a plant that can romp, so give it plenty of room.

RECOMMENDED VARIETIES: 'Atropurpureum' has purple blooms, stems, and leaves. *E. rugosum* 'Chocolate' is a superior ornamental, 3 to 4 feet tall, with a bushy habit, deep reddish-brown leaves, and white flowers in fall. *E. maculatum* 'Gateway' is the most commonly sold. It grows 5 feet high and is spectacular, with purplish-pink flower heads up to 18 inches across and reddish-purple stems.

'Gateway' Joe-Pye weed

GAILLARDIA X GRANDIFLORA

gay-LAR-dee-a gran-di-FLO-ra

Blanket flower

2'
2'

- Perennial
- Zones 3–9
- Flashy, hot colors
- Heat- and drought-tolerant
- Superb cut flowers

Named for the autumnal hues of Native American blankets, this hybrid wildflower of the western United States is a short-lived perennial that blooms all summer and grows from 10 inches to 2 feet tall. The traditional form has red rays with yellow tips.

USES: Good in containers or near the front of beds and borders. Grow with other hot-colored flowers.

CULTURE: Tough and adaptable, it prefers full sun and lean to average soil. Excellent drainage is the key to success; wet clay soils can kill it. Although it will continue to bloom without deadheading, cut off spent blooms to keep plants tidy and promote new growth.

RECOMMENDED VARIETIES: 'Baby Cole' has 2- to 3-inch red-and-yellow flowers on an 8-inch plant. 'Goblin' has 4-inch dark red flowers on a 1-foot plant. 'Burgundy' has a deep wine-red center and streaks. *G. pulchella* 'Red Plume', a heat- and drought-tolerant annual, has double red flowers on an 18- to 20-inch plant.

'Burgundy' blanket flower

GAURA LINDHEIMERI

GOR-ah lind-HY-mer-eye

Gaura

4'
2'

- Short-lived perennial
- Zones 5–9
- Long-lasting white blooms age to pink
- Excellent for weaving through other flowers
- Tolerates heat, humidity, and drought

This 4-foot native wildflower originates in the heat, humidity, and droughts of Louisiana, Texas, and Mexico. Its summer-to-fall blooms make it a valuable garden addition.
USES: Gaura's tall, airy flower spikes look lovely in wild gardens. Although the stems are upright in the beginning of summer, they lean as the growing season wanes. This see-through character makes gaura perfect for the middle or front of the border where it can intertwine with flowers of a denser habit.
CULTURE: Plant in moist, fertile, well-drained garden soil. Gaura likes full sun but will tolerate partial shade. Too much shade and too rich a soil will exaggerate its tendency to lean. Heavy clay soil will kill it. Gaura propagates itself by self-sowing in suitable conditions.
RECOMMENDED VARIETIES: 'Whirling Butterflies' is a shorter version that doesn't flop. 'Siskiyou Pink' is 2 to 3 feet tall with bright pink flowers. 'Corrie's Gold' produces golden variegated leaves and pink flowers on a 3-foot plant.

'Siskiyou Pink' gaura

GAZANIA RIGENS

guh-ZAY-nee-a RIH-genz

Gazania

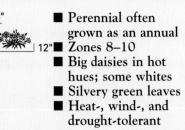

6"
12"

- Perennial often grown as an annual
- Zones 8–10
- Big daisies in hot hues; some whites
- Silvery green leaves
- Heat-, wind-, and drought-tolerant

Gazania's 3- to 4-inch-wide blooms bring bold color to the garden. Red, cream, orange, pink, or yellow ray flowers are streaked, striped, and banded with harmonious colors. These South African natives grow into 6- to 12-inch mounds.
USES: Looks good in containers. An excellent edger, ground cover, bedding, and front-of-the-border plant. Use with 'Mr. Majestic' or 'Safari Red' marigolds, 'Yellow Sun' blanket flower and 'Sonora' gloriosa daisy.
CULTURE: Gazania needs full sun and sandy, light, well-drained soil. It's drought-resistant; water regularly until well established, then only during times of drought. Most varieties benefit from a light application of fertilizer and regular deadheading.
RECOMMENDED VARIETIES: 'Mini-Star Tangerine' is a self-cleaning hybrid with 3-inch, star-shaped flowers on an 8-inch, silvery green mound of leaves. *G. r.* var. *leucolaena* has a more spreading, trailing habit, with yellow, white, orange, or bronze flowers.

'Daybreak Bronze' gazania

GOMPHRENA GLOBOSA

gom-FREE-na glow-BOW-sa

Globe amaranth

18"
12"

- Annual
- Neon shades of red, pink, purple, rose, and white
- Blooms from June to frost
- Excellent for use in fresh and dried arrangements

The flowers of globe amaranth are cloverlike balls that elongate during summer while new flowers are continuously produced. Plants range from 8 inches to 2 feet tall, and flowers are 1 to 2 inches wide.
USES: Globe amaranth is good for containers, cutting gardens, and colorful flower beds. Compact forms work well as edgers and at the front of the border. To dry, cut the flowers before fully open; bunch the stems lightly with a rubber band and hang them upside down in a warm, dark, well-ventilated room to dry.
CULTURE: Grow in light, well-drained garden soil of average fertility in full sun. Water and fertilize lightly. Plants are heat- and drought-tolerant.
RECOMMENDED VARIETIES: 'Strawberry Fields' is bright red. 'Lavender Lady' is lavender. 'Bicolor Rose' has white-centered lilac-rose flowers. 'Buddy Hybrids' have electric deep purple blooms. The 'Gnome' series is best for bedding, with a compact habit only 12 inches high.

'Lavender Lady' globe amaranth

HELENIUM AUTUMNALE

heh-LEE-nee-um aw-tum-NA-lee

Helen's flower

4'

3'

- Perennial
- Zones 3–8
- Yellow, red, orange, and mahogany-red daisies
- Attractive, late-season color
- Tolerates wetness

This sturdy, 3- to 5-foot-tall plant produces 2-inch flowers for about 10 weeks from late summer to fall. Helen's flower is native to wet meadows throughout much of the United States and Canada.

USES: Use in the middle to the back of perennial borders and in wet meadow gardens.

CULTURE: Grow in full sun in moist soil high in organic matter. Divide every 2 to 3 years to keep the plant healthy. Stake plants where necessary. Extreme heat and dry soil sap the plant's vitality.

RECOMMENDED VARIETIES: 'Red and Gold Hybrids' bear red, brown, yellow, and mahogany bicolored flowers on 3-foot plants. 'Moerheim Beauty' produces reddish-bronze flowers that turn orange and gold on 2- to 3-foot plants. 'Goldrausch', a strong 3- to 4-foot plant hardy in Zones 5–8, has yellow-brown blossoms that are good for cutting. 'Butterpat' has rich yellow flowers on 4-foot plants.

'Butterpat' Helen's flower

HELIANTHUS ANNUUS

heh-lee-AN-thus AN-yew-us

Sunflower

7'

3'

- Annual
- Brilliant flowers up to 16 inches wide
- Edible seeds
- Attracts birds and squirrels
- 12-inch dwarfs to 10-foot giants

This cheery flower, a North American native, is adored by people and wildlife alike. Hybrids range from 12 inches to 10 feet tall. Flowers are 4 to 12 inches across in shades of yellow, cream, gold, lemon, bronze, burgundy, mahogany, and brick red.

USES: Make a tall sunflower hedge to block unpleasant views, plant in front of chain-link fences, or grow them for a privacy screen. Use sunflowers along one end of a vegetable garden, in wildlife gardens, and meadow gardens. A must for the children's garden. Dwarf selections make good pot plants, edgers, bedding, and front-of-the-border plants. The flowers are excellent cut for informal arrangements. The seeds are edible.

CULTURE: Sunflowers like light, well-drained soil and full sun but will tolerate most garden soils, light shade, heat, and drought. Stake tall plants in windy areas.

RECOMMENDED VARIETIES: It's fun to try new varieties every year, including 'Velvet Queen', with velvety burgundy and mahogany blooms on a 5-foot plant. 'Chianti' is a similar burgundy with smaller, semidouble flowers. 'Van Gogh Mix' produces 5- to 7-foot plants with single and double flowers 5 to 10 inches wide in cream, lemon, gold, orange, bronze, red, and burgundy. Pollenless, golden yellow flowers with a chartreuse disk make 'Sunbeam' excellent for cutting. Award-winning 'Sonja' has 4- to 6-inch flowers with orange rays and deep brown disks on strong-stemmed, 5- to 6-foot plants. Dwarf 'Teddy Bear' has 6-inch double golden flowers and grows 16 inches tall. 'Supermane' is similar to 'Teddy Bear' but stands up to 8 feet tall and, when planted 4 feet apart, produces a 10-inch central flower and 10 to 40 side branches with smaller sunflowers. 'Big Smile', a dwarf 8 to 24 inches high, has 4- to 6-inch flowers with golden rays and black disks. Heirloom 'Mammoth Russian' has enormous flowers on 9- to 12-foot stalks, making it an ideal bird feeder. *H. maximilianii* is a wild perennial sunflower that grows 6 to 8 feet high and is hardy in Zones 3–9. It produces 3-inch golden yellow flowers on strong stems, making a summer-long floral hedge. It spreads aggressively by seed and underground stems, so use it where you can let it roam.

'Mammoth Russian' sunflower

'Chianti' sunflower

'Teddy Bear' sunflower

HELICHRYSUM BRACTEATUM

heh-LIH-krih-sum brak-tee-AY-tum

Strawflower

- Annual
- Flowers look dazzling fresh or dried
- Available in red, rose, pink, white, bronze, yellow, orange, salmon, burgundy, and more
- Stiff, papery, petal-like bracts

'Bright Bikini' strawflower

If you love colorful flowers from the garden in your house year-round, then strawflowers are a must. Plants vary from 14 inches to 4 feet tall, depending on the variety.

USES: Plant strawflower with other everlastings in cutting or cottage gardens. Cut and dried, strawflowers are excellent in wreaths, crafts, and arrangements.

CULTURE: Strawflowers need full sun and well-drained soil. They benefit from long periods of hot weather. To dry, pick before blossoms are fully open. Cut stems long where possible. Bunch stems, keeping cut ends together with a rubber band. Hang upside down in a dry, dark, warm room with good air circulation until completely dry. Storing or displaying dried strawflowers out of bright sunlight helps maintain color.

RECOMMENDED VARIETIES: 'Bright Bikini Hybrids' have double flowers in bold, hot colors on 14- to 18-inch-tall plants.

HELIOPSIS HELIANTHOIDES

heh-lee-OP-sis heh-lee-an-THOY-deez

False sunflower

- Perennial
- Zones 3–9
- Bright golden daisies
- Long-blooming
- Attracts goldfinches

False sunflower

This vigorous perennial wildflower adds vibrant yellow to the summer garden. The species stands about 4 to 5 feet high; the subspecies *scabra*, 3 feet high, is more compact.

USES: False sunflower looks wonderful in informal garden settings. Mass it in meadow gardens and in perennial borders with tall ornamental grasses and Helen's flower. It is a long-lasting cut flower.

CULTURE: This North American native thrives in full sun and well-drained, moist soil rich in organic matter. The plant is adaptable, however, and will also do well in partial shade and drier conditions. Where summers are wet and very humid, cut down plants if mildew occurs or leaves look tattered. Improve air circulation by thinning. Deadhead to prevent self-sowing; this plant spreads readily by seed.

RECOMMENDED VARIETIES: 'Summer Sun', 3 feet tall, is the most common variety, with double golden flowers. 'Karat' is 4 feet tall with single, intensely golden flowers. 'Loddon Gold' produces an abundance of bright yellow, double, marigoldlike flowers.

HELLEBORUS ORIENTALIS

hel-le-BOW-rus o-ree-en-TA-lis

Lenten rose

- Perennial
- Zones 5–9
- Exotic pink, plum, or white flowers
- Dark, leathery evergreen leaves
- Blooms winter and early spring

Lenten rose

This hardy perennial makes a bold-textured, 2-foot-tall clump that eventually spreads 3 feet wide. Although exotic-looking, its leathery flowers are long-lasting, providing color for 2 months or more in late winter through spring.

USES: Excellent under deciduous trees in beds and borders. It makes a good early-spring cut flower. After cutting, slit stems immediately and condition in cool water.

CULTURE: Grow in light to full shade in moist, well-drained soil high in organic matter. Tolerates a drier and more acid soil than other hellebore species but prefers a neutral to slightly alkaline soil. Once established, it self-sows in good conditions. Plants are poisonous. Crushed leaves produce sap that may irritate the skin.

RECOMMENDED VARIETIES: The Royal Heritage Hybrids tolerate heat, humidity, and clay soil. They bloom in red, white, pink, green, purple, near black, and yellow. *H. foetidus*, bear's foot hellebore, has chartreuse flowers.

HEMEROCALLIS HYBRIDS

heh-mer-oh-KAL-lis

Daylily

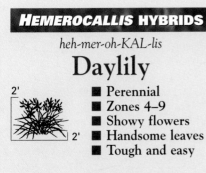

2'

2'

- Perennial
- Zones 4–9
- Showy flowers
- Handsome leaves
- Tough and easy

Daylilies are the consummate easy flower, producing graceful foliage and abundant blooms with the minimum of care. Plants can be evergreen or deciduous, and range from 1 to 5 feet tall. Flowers may be fragrant, bicolored, night- or day-blooming, single, double, or ruffled.

Colors range from yellow and cream through orange, red, and purple.

USES: Wonderful massed in sunny to partly shaded beds and borders, as an edging along a path, and as a sun-loving ground cover. Intermix early-, midseason-, and late-blooming varieties for color all summer. Or grow repeat bloomers for flowers from June until frost.

CULTURE: Grow in sun to part shade in well-drained soil high in organic matter. In the South, give plants afternoon shade. Drought, poor soil, and overly fertilized soil are tolerated but reduce flowering.

RECOMMENDED VARIETIES: Thousands are available. Some of the longest-blooming include

'Happy Returns', a lemon yellow hybrid that repeats from early summer to fall, and 'Stella de Oro' and 'Black Eyed Stella', which bloom nonstop from spring to frost.

'Silent Sentry' daylily, early season

HEUCHERA SPP.

HEW-ker-a

Coral bells

20"

18"

- Perennial
- Zones 3–8
- Airy flower wands
- Long spring and summer bloom
- Ornamental leaves

This North American wildflower attracts hummingbirds with sprays of flowers up to 2 feet high rising from a 6-inch clump of basal leaves.

USES: A staple of perennial borders, rock gardens, wild gardens, and shady beds and slopes, coral

bells makes a delightful see-through edging or front-of-the-border plant and a long-lasting cut flower.

CULTURE: Grow in sun to part shade and in moist, well-drained soil rich in organic matter. Plant about 1 foot apart. Deadheading faded flowers promotes longer bloom.

RECOMMENDED VARIETIES: *H. sanguinea* is the most popular garden species. Choice hybrids include 'Chatterbox', pink; 'June Bride', white; 'Raspberry Regal', rose-red; and 'Mt. St. Helens', cardinal red. *H. micrantha* 'Pewter Moon' has pink flowers on maroon stems with silvery foliage above and maroon below. 'Palace Purple' has creamy flowers and dark purple leaves that fade to

greenish bronze. × *Heucherella*, a cross between coral bells and foam flower, has long-blooming flowers and marbled leaves. 'Bridget Bloom' has pink flowers from late spring through summer.

'Raspberry Regal' coral bells

HIBISCUS SYRIACUS

hih-BISS-kus sih-ree-AY-kus

Rose of Sharon

12'

10'

- Deciduous shrub or small tree
- Zones 5–8
- Pink, white, violet-blue; blooms July through September

This upright shrub or small tree grows up to 12 feet high and 10 feet wide with single or double flowers up to 4 inches wide.

USES: Grow Rose of Sharon in shrub or mixed borders, masses, informal hedges, or for a spot of late-

season color at the foundation.

CULTURE: Grow in full sun to partial shade in moist, well-drained soil rich in organic matter. It likes heat but will die in very dry soils. Rose of Sharon flowers on new wood; prune stems hard in early spring to stimulate flowering. It often self-sows.

RECOMMENDED VARIETIES: 'Diana' has large white flowers, dark green leaves, and a long season of bloom. 'Sky Blue' has blue flowers from July to frost. 'Minerva' has abundant dark red-eyed lavender flowers up to 5 inches wide from June to September. *H. moscheutos*, rose mallow, is a hardy perennial with huge, dinner-plate blooms from late summer to frost on husky plants 4 to

6 feet tall. It is tolerant of wet soils. 'Lord Baltimore' has 10-inch red flowers; 'Blue River' is white. The 'Southern Belle' series is more compact, 3 to 4 feet tall.

'Aphrodite' Rose of Sharon

HYDRANGEA SPP.

hy-DRAN-jee-uh

Hydrangea

'Nikko Blue' bigleaf hydrangea

Oakleaf hydrangea

4'

7'

- Deciduous shrubs
- Zones 3–9, depending on species
- Late-season flowers
- Long bloom period
- Terrific border plant

From shade-tolerant shrubs to vines and small trees, there's a hydrangea for every shady garden. Varieties range from 3 to 20 feet high, and a vine that can climb 80 feet.

USES: Hydrangeas look impressive massed in the border, at the foundation, or as a specimen. The climbing species looks handsome growing on trees or brick walls. Potted hydrangeas add charm to a stone or brick patio.

CULTURE: Hydrangeas can tolerate full sun but prefer partial shade. They thrive in moist, well-drained soil rich in organic matter.

RECOMMENDED VARIETIES: Climbing hydrangea, *H. petiolaris*, is a deciduous woody vine with attractive brown peeling bark and white lace-cap flowers up to 10 inches wide in summer. False climbing hydrangea, *Schizophragma hydrangeoides*, is nearly identical except somewhat later blooming. Smooth hydrangea, *H. arborescens*, is a 3- to 5-foot shrub with white flowers. 'Annabelle' has huge 1-foot flower heads over a long season in midsummer. Bigleaf hydrangea, *H. macrophylla*, grows 3 to 10 feet tall in Zones 6–9. It blooms midsummer to fall. Acid soils with a pH of 5.0–5.5 cause the flowers to become blue; alkaline soils with a pH of 6.0–6.5 produce pink flowers. 'Blue Wave' has blue lace-cap flowers. 'Nikko Blue' has blue, rounded "mop-head" flowers. 'Pia' has a dwarf, 2-foot habit and flowers that remain pink in all soils. Many other good cultivars are available. Oakleaf hydrangea, *H. quercifolia* 'Snowflake', 4 to 8 feet tall, has double flowers that turn from white to dusky pink and then tan. Its peeling bark and oaklike leaves, which turn red, orange, or purple in fall, add to its year-round beauty. 'Snow Queen' bears profuse, larger, and more erect panicles.

IMPATIENS WALLERIANA

im-PAY-shunz wal-le-RA-na

Impatiens

12"

10"

- Annual
- America's favorite shade bedding plant
- Summer-long color
- Available in red, pink, white, coral, orange, and bicolors
- Low, mounded habit

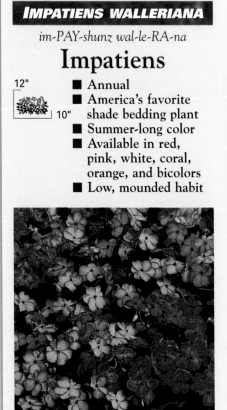

'Super Elfin Twilight' impatiens

This shade-loving plant, a native of eastern Africa, enlivens dark garden corners with brilliant color from early summer to the first frost. It grows 6 to 18 inches high with flowers up to 2 inches wide.

USES: Impatiens is an excellent choice for containers and hanging baskets, for edging paths and borders, at the foundation, and for bedding. It is most effective planted in masses. Combine the colorful flowers of impatiens with ferns, ivy, hostas, coral bells, and other shade-loving plants with outstanding foliage.

CULTURE: Plant impatiens about 18 inches apart after the last frost. Impatiens prefers moist, well-drained, humusy soil in partial to full shade but takes more sun in cool-summer locations. Regular but light applications of fertilizer benefit the plant, making it grow bigger and more floriferous.

RECOMMENDED VARIETIES: The 'Super Elfin' series offers a huge range of colors on compact plants bred for bedding. 'Red Velvet Super Elfin' has bronze leaves and red flowers. 'Super Elfin Twilight' bears sparkling light pink flowers with deep rose picotee edges. The award-winning 'Mosaic' series produces rose, lilac, or violet flowers with subtle "thumbprints" of soft, streaky white at the petal centers. The 'Pride' series bears exceptionally large, 2½-inch blossoms on compact plants perfect for bedding. It offers a wide variety of colors and bicolors. 'Victorian Rose' has rose-shaped 1-inch semidouble flowers. 'Confection Hybrids' has double flowers in orange, rose, and red with dark green leaves and a bushy habit. The New Guinea group of hybrid impatiens has flowers up to 2½ inches wide and attractive leaves that can be variegated or tinged with purple. They tolerate more sun than other impatiens. 'Tango Improved' is 2 feet tall and 18 inches wide with brilliant orange blooms; the 'Java' series has 2-inch flowers and includes bicolor 'Java Lilac Flame', 'Java Orange Flame', 'Java Cherry Rose', and 'Java Pink'.

IPOMOEA ALBA

ih-poh-MEE-uh AL-buh

Moonflower

15'
2'

- Annual twining vine
- Big fragrant white flowers
- Night-blooming

Moonflower, a tender perennial usually grown as an annual, climbs 10 to 20 feet in a summer. Perfumed flowers 6 to 8 inches wide open in late afternoon against large, dark green, tropical-appearing leaves.

USES: Plant moonflower near doors, paths, patios, and windows—anyplace where you can appreciate its sweet scent at night.

CULTURE: Moonflower prefers full sun and average moisture. Soak seed overnight before sowing directly in the garden after the last frost. Plants grow slowly in cool weather, more quickly when the weather is hot.

RECOMMENDED VARIETIES: Other ornamental relatives include *I. × multifida*, cardinal climber, with red flowers that bloom all day and attract hummingbirds. *I. quamoclit*, cypress vine, is similar, with red trumpet flowers and feathery, ferny leaves. *I. tricolor*, morning glory, is a vigorous, popular vine with bold blue, pink, white, or bicolored flowers that open on sunny days. 'Heavenly Blue' is a reliable blue variety. *I. batatas*, sweet potato vine, is an attractive trailing foliage plant for containers and bedding. 'Marguarite' has bright chartreuse leaves; 'Blackie' has deep maroon, almost black, leaves.

Moonflower

IRIS SIBIRICA

EYE-ris sy-BEE-ri-kuh

Siberian iris

3'
2'

- Perennial
- Zones 3–9
- Rich colors from blue and purple to yellow and white
- Fine grassy foliage
- Adaptable

This handsome iris produces 3-inch flowers that bloom in late spring and stand above clumps of upright, arching leaves. Clumps are about 2 feet wide and 2 to 4 feet tall, depending on growing conditions.

USES: Grow Siberian iris in the perennial border. Plant in masses as an edging or in clumps of two or three plants of the same variety.

CULTURE: Siberian iris thrives in full sun to light shade and in either poor or rich soils. It tolerates both dry and wet soils well but grows best and tallest in rich, moist, acid soil full of organic matter. Divide in early spring or fall when the number of blooms drops.

RECOMMENDED VARIETIES: 'Caesar's Brother' is violet-blue. 'White Swirl' is a lovely white, 'Heavenly Blue' a good, pure blue. *I. pseudacorus*, yellow flag, is a 4-foot, yellow-flowered native good for wet or soggy soil. *I. ensata*, Japanese iris, is a 5-foot plant with large, flat flowers. Grow it in rich, moist, acid soil or in shallow water.

'Blue Moon' Siberian iris

LAMIUM MACULATUM

LAY-mee-yum mak-you-LAY-tum

Spotted dead nettle

6"
18"

- Perennial
- Zones 3–8
- Pink or white flowers
- Silver and green leaves
- Vigorous ground cover

Once established, this hardy ground cover blooms intermittently all season long, with the biggest flush of bloom from late spring to midsummer. Plants grow 4 to 12 inches high and spread 18 inches.

USES: Spotted dead nettle is an excellent ground cover for shady places. Its variegated leaves perk up dark spots under trees, at the front of beds and borders, and in foundation plantings. Grow with fringed bleeding heart and hostas.

CULTURE: Prefers partial to full shade in moist, well-drained soil rich in organic matter, but tolerates sandy soils. Keep shaded and well-watered in the South; it is not drought-tolerant. Lamium spreads by rhizomes and also roots where it touches the ground. To increase plantings, divide it in spring or fall.

RECOMMENDED VARIETIES: 'White Nancy' has white flowers, 'Red Nancy' has silver leaves and red flowers, 'Beedham's White' has white flowers and chartreuse leaves, and 'Beacon Silver' has pink flowers and spotted silver leaves.

'Beacon Silver' spotted dead nettle

LANTANA CAMARA

lan-TA-nuh ka-MAH-ruh

Lantana

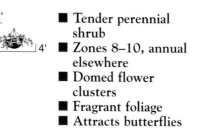
2'
4'

- Tender perennial shrub
- Zones 8–10, annual elsewhere
- Domed flower clusters
- Fragrant foliage
- Attracts butterflies

A tender perennial usually grown as an annual, lantana is actually a rounded shrub that grows up to 6 feet high and blooms from summer to frost in the North and year-round in warmer regions.

USES: This is an excellent container plant and a colorful addition to beds and borders. Use in butterfly gardens and potted on sunny decks and patios. Plant with verbena, cosmos, and flossflower with a background of canna and Mexican sunflower.

CULTURE: Grow in rich, moist, well-drained soil in full sun. Pinching young growing tips makes a bushier plant. Once established, lantana tolerates heat, drought, and salt. It is excellent for seaside plantings.

RECOMMENDED VARIETIES: 'Patriot Hybrids' is a popular new series that comes in a wide range of color. 'Boston Gold' (syn. 'Aloha') has gold flowers with gold-variegated leaves. 'Feston Rose' opens yellow and turns dark rosy pink. *L. montevidensis* has pink-and-lilac flowers and a spreading, trailing habit excellent for hanging baskets.

'Tangerine' lantana

LAVANDULA ANGUSTIFOLIA

luh-VAN-dew-luh
an-goose-ti-FOH-lee-uh

English lavender

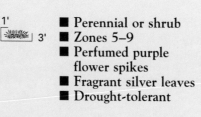
1'
3'

- Perennial or shrub
- Zones 5–9
- Perfumed purple flower spikes
- Fragrant silver leaves
- Drought-tolerant

Cultivated for its exquisite scent and long-lasting flower spikes, this Mediterranean shrub grows up to 2 feet high and 3 feet wide.

USES: Grow it in herb gardens and silver gardens. It makes an attractive low hedge in parterres and a fine-textured edging for beds and borders. The edible flowers flavor ices, cakes, and *herbes de Provence*. Lavender is useful for crafts and potpourris.

CULTURE: Lavender grows best in full sun and well-drained, somewhat dry or sandy soil with a neutral to alkaline pH. Cut back flower stems after blooming. In cold climates prune plants hard in spring after new growth appears to prevent a straggly form. In warm areas, trim lavender at any time of year to keep it in shape. Lavender tolerates heat and drought, but overwatering can kill it.

RECOMMENDED VARIETIES: 'Hidcote' grows 2 feet tall with dark violet-blue flowers. 'Munstead', hardy in Zones 6–9, grows 1 to 2 feet tall with deep purple flowers. 'Rosea' and 'Miss Katharine' have pink flowers. Compact 'Alba' and 'Nana Alba' have white flowers.

'Martha Roderick' English lavender

LAVATERA TRIMESTRIS

la-va-TARE-uh try-MESS-tris

Tree mallow

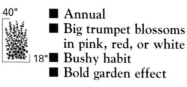
40"
18"

- Annual
- Big trumpet blossoms in pink, red, or white
- Bushy habit
- Bold garden effect

Tree mallow adds not only color but also mass to the garden. It has a branching, shrubby form and grows from 2 to 5 feet tall and 1 to 2 feet wide. Its hollyhocklike flowers grow to 4 inches across.

USES: Cultivate toward the back of beds and borders. Its size and all-summer bloom make it an excellent filler for bare spots and for bringing temporary color to the shrub border. Cut entire branches for bouquets.

CULTURE: Plant this annual after the last frost, setting plants about 18 inches apart in full sun and in well-drained, humusy garden soil. Keep well watered. Monthly applications of low-nitrogen fertilizer encourage abundant flowering. Plants will self-sow in good conditions.

RECOMMENDED VARIETIES: 'Loveliness' is 3 to 4 feet tall and dark pink. Shorter, 2- to 3-foot selections are 'Mont Blanc', white; 'Mont Rose', pink; and 'Silver Cup', pink. 'Dwarf White Cherub' is 14 inches high. *L. thuringiaca* is a long-blooming shrubby perennial in Zones 6–9 with pink or white flowers. 'Barnsley' has fringed white flowers fading to pink with red eyes.

'Mont Rose' tree mallow

LEPTOSPERMUM SCOPARIUM

lep-toh-SPUR-mum sko-PAR-ee-um

New Zealand tea-tree

10'
6'

- Evergreen shrub or small tree
- Zones 9–10
- Red, pink, or white flowers late winter through spring
- Fragrant leaves

New Zealand tea-tree ranges from a 10-foot shrub to an 8-inch ground cover. A New Zealand native, it's excellent for West Coast gardens. In the North it's lovely in containers.

USES: Needlelike leaves give this shrub a fine texture in the garden. Grow tall forms as an accent in the shrub border, in masses, or alone as a garden specimen or focal point. Low forms make a colorful ground cover but are not dense enough to suppress weeds.

CULTURE: Drought-tolerant and pest-free, this plant thrives in full sun and fast-draining soil. Avoid pruning to bare wood, which prevents buds from breaking into new growth.

RECOMMENDED VARIETIES: 'Ruby Glow' has double red flowers and dark leaves and is 6 to 8 feet tall. 'Nanum' has single pink flowers with dark red centers on a 2-foot shrub. 'Red Damask' has double cerise, long-lasting flowers on a 6- to 8-foot shrub. 'Snow White' is a 3-foot shrub with white flowers from December through March.

'Nanum' New Zealand tea-tree

LILIUM HYBRIDS

LI-lee-um

Lily

4'
1'

- Perennial bulb
- Zones 3–9, depending on variety
- Classic blooms in every color but blue
- Good for cutting

Perennial garden favorites, lilies bear flowers 1 to 10 inches wide on 1- to 8-foot-tall plants. Although individual lilies have relatively short bloom seasons, by combining varieties you can extend the bloom from late May to early September.

USES: Lilies bring elegance and sometimes a sweet perfume to bouquets. They add beauty to herbaceous and mixed borders.

CULTURE: Plant at a depth about three times the height of the bulb in early spring or fall. Grow in groups of three or more with bulbs planted about 1 foot apart in full sun to partial shade in moist, fertile, well-drained soil rich in organic matter. Snap off fading flowers, but do not cut back leaves or stems until they have yellowed.

RECOMMENDED VARIETIES: Thousands of cultivars exist. Popular hybrids include early-blooming Asiatics such as white 'Mont Blanc' and pink 'Gypsy'; tall midseason Aurelian 'Thunderbolt' with apricot blooms; and fragrant pink-and-white 'Stargazer' and white 'Casa Blanca' Oriental lilies.

'Enchantment' hybrid Asiatic lily

LIMONIUM LATIFOLIUM

li-MOH-nee-um la-tih-FOLE-ee-um

Sea lavender

2'
2'

- Perennial
- Zones 3–9
- Airy stems of lavender flowers in mid- to late summer
- Salt-tolerant

This plant, with a bushy yet see-through habit, grows 2 feet high and wide. Upright stems rise from a clump of big, leathery, green basal leaves that turn bright red in fall.

USES: Sea lavender looks lovely massed in seaside plantings, in the midborder, and in fresh or dried cut flower arrangements. Plant with ornamental grasses, yucca, and prostrate rosemary.

CULTURE: Grow in full sun to part shade in well-drained, sandy soil of average fertility. Do not overwater. Limonium is both salt- and heat-tolerant. To dry flowers, cut just before they are fully open when the color is fresh; tie stems together with a rubber band, and hang upside down in a dark, warm, dry place with good air circulation.

RECOMMENDED VARIETIES: *L. perezii* is a similar but tender perennial (Zones 8–11) useful in beach plantings in California. *L. sinuatum* is an annual grown for use as a fresh or dried cut flower; it has winged stems with little papery blooms. 'Blue Bonnet' is sky blue, 'American Beauty' is dark rose, 'Iceberg' is white, and 'Friendly Yellow' is bright yellow.

Sea lavender

LINUM PERENNE

LYE-num pur-REN

Perennial flax

Perennial flax

18"

12"

- Perennial
- Zones 5–8
- Masses of sky blue flowers open daily
- Linear gray-green leaves
- Delicate texture

This drought-tolerant European native produces profuse blue blooms from late spring through summer. The blooms open only on sunny days, and close by afternoon. Its fragile, willowy stature, 1 to 2 feet high and 1 foot wide, belies a tough nature that needs little care.

USES: The bright blue flowers enhance rock gardens, wild gardens, and borders. Grow it with pink evening primrose and annual phlox.

CULTURE: Plant in full sun and well-drained, sandy soil. It self-sows freely once established. Too much winter wetness can kill it.

RECOMMENDED VARIETIES: 'Blue Sapphire' has blue flowers 1 inch wide on a dwarf 8- to 12-inch plant, making it particularly good for rock gardens. 'Diamant' is white and 16 inches high. Low-growing *L. p.* ssp. *alpinum* has 1-inch pure blue flowers on 9- to 12-inch trailing stems and is hardy to Zone 4. *L. narbonense* 'Heavenly Blue' has longer-lasting, deep blue flowers that close in the afternoon. *L. grandiflorum*, an annual, has white, red, pink, or purple blooms on a plant 15 to 24 inches high.

LOBULARIA MARITIMA

lah-bew-LAY-ree-a may-ri-TEE-ma

Sweet alyssum

'Oriental Night' sweet alyssum

4"

12"

- Annual
- Clouds of tiny, fragrant white, pink, and lavender flowers
- Low, spreading mound
- Blooms spring to frost
- Self-sows freely

This trailing annual offers fuss-free color from spring to frost. Delicate leaves, diminutive blooms, and a low habit (4 to 6 inches high) give it a fine texture in the landscape.

USES: Sweet alyssum is perfect for rock gardens and cottage gardens, and as edging along paths and at the front of beds. Tucked in cracks and crevices, it lends country charm to stone walls or walks.

CULTURE: Grow in full sun to part shade in ordinary, well-drained soil, but it tolerates some drought and a wide range of soils. For best performance, keep it watered. Tends to stop blooming in hot weather; cut it back for rebloom in fall.

RECOMMENDED VARIETIES: 'Snowcloth', 4 inches tall, blooms early with a dense cover of pure white flowers. 'Royal Carpet', 4 inches high and 10 inches wide, has violet blooms. 'Oriental Night' has rich purple blooms on 4-inch plants. 'Wonderland Deep Rose' has deep rose flowers on 3-inch plants. 'Easter Basket Hybrids' have flowers in pink, rose, violet, lavender, or white on 4-inch plants.

LONICERA SEMPERVIRENS

lo-NI-se-ruh sem-per-VYE-renz

Trumpet honeysuckle

Trumpet honeysuckle

12'

4'

- Deciduous woody twining vine
- Zones 4–9
- Showy red trumpets
- Blooms spring to fall
- Tubular blooms attract hummingbirds

This vine climbs by twining to reach 10 to 15 feet high. Native to the United States, it produces unscented red-orange flowers followed by berries loved by birds.

USES: Grow on trellises, arches, or arbors. Also beautifies fences, bamboo tripods, and lattice.

CULTURE: Honeysuckle prefers full sun but can take deep shade, though flowering will be sparse. Grow in moist, well-drained, acid to neutral soil. Prune right after flowering; cutting it back in late winter will remove next season's blooms.

RECOMMENDED VARIETIES: 'John Clayton' has abundant yellow flowers and red fruit. 'Cedar Lane' has lavish, dark red, repeat-blooming flowers. *L. flava* is a native yellow honeysuckle with red berries in late summer. *L.× heckrottii*, goldflame honeysuckle, has fragrant maroon flowers with a yellow interior. *L. periclymenum* 'Serotina' grows 15 to 20 feet tall and bears heavily fragrant pink flowers with creamy interiors all summer long. 'Graham Thomas' has fragrant creamy yellow flowers.

LUNARIA ANNUA

lew-NAY-ree-a AN-new-uh

Money plant

2'
2'

- Annual or biennial
- Zones 4–8
- Self-sows freely
- Purple flowers
- Seedpods resemble translucent coins

This old-fashioned biennial produces coarse leaves and flower spikes 1 to 3 feet tall. After flowering in May, flat, round seedpods up to 2 inches wide develop for picking in August.
USES: Because it self-sows and can look rangy by summer's end, money plant is best in wild gardens, cutting gardens, or an informal flower bed, where you can enjoy it before harvesting the dry seedpods. The moonlike disks from money plant's seedpods make magical additions to fresh and dried arrangements.
CULTURE: Once established, money plant self-sows freely. It's not picky about site, preferring full sun and well-drained soil rich in organic matter but tolerating drought, poor soil, and partial shade.
RECOMMENDED VARIETIES:
'Alba' has white flowers. 'Variegata' has variegated leaves and red-purple flowers. *L. rediviva* is a moisture-loving perennial with light lavender flowers in early summer followed by attractive, flattened oval seedpods. It grows 3 to 4 feet tall.

'Variegata' money plant

LYCORIS SQUAMIGERA

lye-KOH-ris skwa-MIH-je-ruh

Hardy amaryllis

24"
12"

- Perennial bulb
- Zones 5–9
- Strap-shaped leaves emerge and disappear in spring
- Lilylike pink blooms in late summer on tall, bare stems
- Fragrant

Hardy amaryllis, also known as naked lady, resurrection lily, and magic lily, has short-lived spring leaves that give no hint of the lovely scented flowers that follow in August on long stems. Each bulb produces 2-foot stems topped by a cluster of up to 8 blooms, each 4 inches long. Native to Japan.
USES: Plant in the woodland garden or border with ground cover plants that hide the dying leaves in spring and enhance or fill out its naked base in bloom.
CULTURE: Plant the bulbs, which are 2 to 3 inches wide, 6 inches deep in full sun to part shade in average, well-drained soil.
RECOMMENDED VARIETIES:
L. radiata (Zones 7–9) has feathery red blooms on 20-inch stems with leaves that appear after flowering and last through the winter.

Hardy amaryllis

MANDEVILLA X AMABILIS

man-duh-VIL-la a-MAH-bi-lis

Mandevilla

12'
4'

- Tender evergreen twining vine often grown as an annual
- Zone 10
- Showy, pink trumpets summer to frost

This vigorous, twining climber grows up to 15 feet in a season. It produces nonstop 3- to 4-inch-wide blossoms that open light pink and turn deep rose. Even without its blooms, this plant would be worth growing for its large, gleaming leaves. It is a tropical perennial grown as an annual in the North.
USES: In pots mandevilla enlivens patios and decks with height and summer color. Provide support (trellis, lattice, or fence) when growing in containers or in the ground.
CULTURE: Plant in full sun or partial shade in moist, rich soil. Fertilize every few weeks to keep it blooming. To keep it tidy, trim long shoots or weave them into the support on which it grows. Bring indoors for the winter and grow in a cool, bright location. Prune hard before setting it out again in spring.
RECOMMENDED VARIETIES:
'Alice du Pont' bears pink flowers with dark throats. 'Janell' has lavish rosy red flowers; 'Leah' is blush pink. 'Red Riding Hood' (dark pink) grows shorter and is good for short trellises and hanging baskets.

'Alice du Pont' mandevilla

MIRABILIS JALAPA

mih-RAH-bi-lis jah-LAH-pah

Four-o-clock

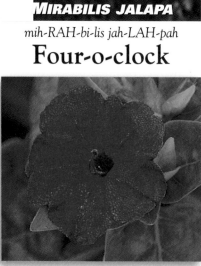

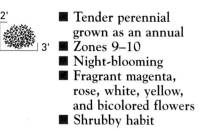
2'
3'

- Tender perennial grown as an annual
- Zones 9–10
- Night-blooming
- Fragrant magenta, rose, white, yellow, and bicolored flowers
- Shrubby habit

Four-o-clock flowers in late afternoon as many tired commuters come home from work. A tender perennial grown as an annual, it forms a 3-foot clump and is native to tropical America.
USES: Grow this plant in the evening garden for its powerful night perfume. Like flowering tobacco, it works well in beds and

'Red Glow' four-o-clock

containers near doors, windows, patios, paths, and decks. It can also function as a temporary shrub or barrier, because it grows quickly and blooms from summer to frost.
CULTURE: Grow in full sun to part shade in any soil. Propagate plants from seed or the tuberous roots, which grow big in hot climates.
RECOMMENDED VARIETIES: 'Kaleidoscope' bears flowers splashed in red, pink, orange, yellow, and white. 'Jingles' has flowers striped in yellow, red, rose, white, pink, and salmon, with different colored flowers on the same plant. 'Tea Time' is 24 inches high with flowers that open earlier than the species.

MISCANTHUS SINENSIS

miss-KAN-thus sih-NEN-siss

Miscanthus

5'
3'

- Perennial grass
- Zones 5–9
- Large pink or silver plumes in fall
- Winter interest

This outstanding grass—valued for its foliage, flowers, and seed heads—forms dense clumps that grow 3 to 7 feet tall.
USES: Excellent in the back of the border and as a specimen, either massed or solitary. Because its foliage emerges late in spring or early summer, it makes a good companion for spring-blooming ephemerals such as bulbs.
CULTURE: Free of pests and diseases, this low-maintenance

'Sarabande' miscanthus

plant, when established with moderate watering, requires little attention. Best in full sun (it flops in shade) in average to heavy soil. It likes moderately moist conditions, although it tolerates drought well. Allow 4 to 5 feet between plants. Cut back in late winter or early spring before new growth begins.
RECOMMENDED VARIETIES: Many cultivars are available. 'Gracillimus' is the most common; it grows 3 to 4 feet tall with silvery plumes and narrow, curly leaves. Flame grass, 'Purpurascens', has orange-red fall color and silvery plumes. 'Sarabande' is a choice fine-textured selection with silvery plumes and an upright habit.

MONARDA DIDYMA 'MARSHALL'S DELIGHT'

moh-NAR-duh DID-y-muh

Bee balm

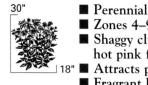
30"
18"

- Perennial
- Zones 4–9
- Shaggy clusters of hot pink flowers
- Attracts pollinators
- Fragrant leaves

Bees, butterflies, and hummingbirds delight in bee balm's summer blooms. Easy and vigorous, it grows 3 to 4 feet high and forms a clump that spreads rapidly in good soil.
USES: Massed bee balm suits wild gardens and open meadows that are mowed once a year. It is a good cut flower and can be dried by hanging upside down in a warm, dry place.
CULTURE: Bee balm prefers full sun to partial shade and moist, rich soil

'Marshall's Delight' bee balm

for maximum bloom. It's adaptable, however, to other soils, where it will be shorter and less floriferous. Most bee balms are susceptible to powdery mildew; provide adequate air circulation to help prevent the disease. Dig up the plant and divide it if it stops blooming in the center. Cut off the older portions and discard; replant outer pieces 1 foot apart.
RECOMMENDED VARIETIES: The pink 'Marshall's Delight' is highly resistant to mildew. Other resistant varieties include dwarf 'Petite Delight', a 1- to 2-foot-tall plant with rosy pink flowers; and 'Panorama Red Shades', a rich vermilion. 'Jacob Kline' is the best red, very resistant to mildew.

MYOSOTIS SYLVATICA

my-oh-SOH-tis sil-VA-ti-kah

Forget-me-not

- Biennial
- Unforgettable sky blue flowers
- Compact habit
- Spring-blooming

Bright blue forget-me-nots are emblems of spring. Growing 6 to 15 inches tall, they are native to Europe and Asia and are also available in pink and white.

USES: Grow forget-me-nots massed around spring bulbs. Daffodils and tulips look stunning in a sea of its tiny flowers. Forget-me-nots are lovely in sunny and shady beds and borders, under trees, in woodland or boggy areas, and crowded in window boxes with pansies and violas.

CULTURE: Grows well in sun or shade in moist, nutrient-rich, well-drained, cool soil. Sow directly in the garden in late summer or early fall for blooms the next spring. It tolerates wetness and self-sows abundantly.

RECOMMENDED VARIETIES: Although the species looks leggy by spring's end, new selections have a more compact, mounded habit. 'Victoria Blue' has intense blue flowers on moisture-loving, 6- to 8-inch plants that bloom in May and June. 'Royal Blue Improved' bears indigo blue flowers on a 12-inch plant.

'Ultra Marine' forget-me-not

NARCISSUS HYBRIDS

nar-SIS-sus

Daffodil

- Perennial bulb
- Zones 3–9, depending on the variety
- Old-fashioned emblems of spring
- Yellow, white, pink, orange, and bicolored flowers
- Distasteful to deer and most squirrels; bulbs are poisonous

A cluster of blooming daffodils brings cheer and warmth to any garden in spring. Daffodils range from 4 to 20 inches tall and produce flowers from 1½ to 4½ inches wide. Most species are native to the mountains of Spain, Portugal, France, and northern Africa, but the thousands of varieties grown in modern gardens are usually of hybrid origin.

USES: Daffodils look best planted in sweeps on grassy hillsides or in borders under deciduous trees and shrubs. Small varieties are excellent in rock gardens. Single varieties planted in masses with several yards of lawn or woodland in between look lush but natural. 'Tete-a-Tete' and paper whites are popular for forcing indoors for winter blooms. Grow them with daylilies in sun or with ferns and hellebores in deciduous shade to hide the fading leaves. Grow early-, mid-, and late-season bulbs for almost 3 months of continuous bloom in your garden. Superb cut flowers.

CULTURE: Excellent drainage is the key to success with daffodils, which like sun to partial shade. They tolerate most soils but heavy ones, so if your soil is clay, dig in peat, compost, or leaf mold to improve drainage. Plant bulbs in fall anytime before the ground freezes to a depth of three times the bulb's height and about 4 to 12 inches apart, depending on whether the daffodil is miniature, medium, or full size. Plant the pointed side of the bulb facing the sky and the flatter root side down. After flowering, do not cut, braid, or tie up the foliage while green, because this hurts the bulbs' growth.

RECOMMENDED VARIETIES: 'Kassels Gold', 18 inches, blooms early and for a long time. 'Barrett Browning' is pure white with a small reddish cup in early season. 'Thalia', 15 inches, produces 3 milky white, fragrant, old-fashioned flowers per stem in midspring. 'Actaea', 16 inches, flowers in late spring with scented white petals surrounding a flat, red-rimmed, yellow cup. 'Minnow' produces small, very fragrant white flowers with yellow cups in early spring. 'Tete-a-Tete' is a 10-inch miniature yellow that blooms in early spring with the crocuses. 'Jack Snipe', 9 inches, has white reflexed petals and a narrow yellow trumpet.

'Brent' daffodil

'Barrett Browning' daffodil

'Tete-a-Tete' cyclamen daffodil

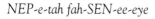

NEPETA X FAASSENII

NEP-e-tah fah-SEN-ee-eye

Catmint

18"

18"

- ■ Perennial
- ■ Zones 4–9
- ■ Light blue flowers
- ■ Long-blooming
- ■ Good lavender substitute

'Six Hills Giant' catmint

Sometimes called the poor man's lavender, catmint forms durable, spreading, 2-foot mounds of tiny gray-green leaves covered with wands of pale blue flowers that bees love. It blooms from late spring to midsummer; if cut back it blooms until fall. The parents of this hybrid species come from North Africa and the Caucasus.

USES: Catmint keeps blooming long after other late-spring perennials have stopped. Use it as a sun-loving flowering ground cover. Or plant it in drifts in the border or rock garden, to soften a path's edge, or to fill in edged geometric beds in the herb garden. A member of the mint family, it has fragrant leaves that can be used in potpourris and flowers that are good for bouquets.

CULTURE: Catmint prefers well-drained soil in full sun. Once established, it tolerates some heat and drought. Extremely rich, moist, partly shaded soil may induce catmint to sprawl. Most catmint species form spreading clumps and self-sow. *N.* × *faassenii*, however,

is a sterile hybrid with a neater habit. To encourage rebloom later in the summer, cut *N.* × *faassenii* back by half in July after flowering. If you grow *N. cataria*, catnip, take care not to crush leaves or stems when doing garden maintenance. The scent attracts cats, which may frolic in the plant until they destroy it.

RECOMMENDED VARIETIES: 'Alba' has white flowers and grows 1 to 2 feet high. 'Dropmore' sports big, dark lavender flowers. 'Six Hills Giant' grows 2 to 3 feet tall with deep lavender-blue flowers and bigger leaves. 'Walker's Low' is 10 inches tall spreading to 3 feet wide, with prolific lilac-blue flowers and aromatic gray-green leaves. 'Blue Ice' is 1 foot tall and 1½ feet wide, with ice blue blooms marked with white. 'Blue Wonder' is a compact 15 inches by 15 inches. *N. sibirica* 'Blue Beauty' (also known as 'Souvenir d'Andre Chaudron') is upright, to 3 feet tall, with violet flowers and summer-long bloom. *N. nervosa* 'Blue Carpet' is a 10-inch ground cover with violet flowers that bloom all summer long.

NICOTIANA ALATA

nih-koh-she-AH-nuh a-LAY-tuh

Jasmine tobacco

2'

1'

- ■ Annual
- ■ Creamy white tubular flowers
- ■ Intensely fragrant
- ■ Night-blooming

This Brazilian native has white flower trumpets with star-shaped tips that open at night to release their

'Metro Mix' flowering tobacco

powerful perfume. Leaves are hairy and sticky. A tender perennial usually treated as an annual, it grows 3 to 4 feet tall with a narrow, graceful habit, and blooms from early summer to frost.

USES: Grow it along paths, in containers, under open windows, near doors and patios, or anywhere you may be in the evening or at night. Use it with cosmos to fill in borders left empty by early-blooming perennials. Tall varieties make excellent back-of-the-border plants.

CULTURE: Easy to grow in moist, well-drained soil in full sun to part shade. Tolerates heat and humidity but grows well in cool climates. Self-sows freely. Keep pets and children away from the leaves, which are poisonous. Plant smaller varieties 1 to 2 feet apart and larger types 2 to 2½ feet apart.

RECOMMENDED VARIETIES: 'Daylight Hybrids' have blooms that stay open by day. 'Fragrant Cloud' reaches 3 feet high with powerful nighttime fragrance. Langsdorf's tobacco, *N. langsdorffii*, grows 3 to

5 feet tall with lime green, bell-shaped, unscented blooms. Woodland tobacco, *N. sylvestris*, is a dramatic annual for shade or part shade, with fragrant, white, airy clusters of flowers on 4-foot stalks that emerge from huge, tropical-appearing basal leaves; 'Only the Lonely' grows 4 to 5 feet, with clusters of 20 to 30 white tubular flowers 3 to 4 inches long and big leaves up to 2 feet in length and 1 foot wide. *N.* × *sanderae* is the familiar flowering tobacco available as many cultivars for bedding in sun or part shade. Most are not fragrant, but the 'Heaven Scent' series has 2- to 3-foot bushy plants with fragrant red, rose, purple, and white flowers. The 'Nicki' series flowers earlier with more compact branching; the 'Metro' series is similar with 14-inch plants. The 'Havana' series is 12 to 14 inches high with several unusual colors, including the elegant 'Havana Appleblossom' and 'Havana Lime Green'. 'Domino Hybrids' are 14-inch plants with 2½-inch flowers in a wide variety of colors.

NIGELLA DAMASCENA

nye-JEL-luh dam-as-SEE-nuh

Love-in-a-mist

18"
18"

- Annual
- True-blue flowers
- See-through foliage
- Excellent cut and dried

This old-fashioned favorite, a native of southern Europe, stands 1½ to 3 feet high. Cultivated for cottage-garden appeal, it's easy to grow and blooms from early to midsummer.
USES: Love-in-a-mist weaves and leans to complement plants with a denser habit such as coreopsis. Massed in the garden, it forms cloudlike areas of ferny leaves punctuated by striking blooms, which make long-lasting cut flowers. Seed capsules, shaped like eggs and covered with branching spines, are equally ornamental.
CULTURE: Sow directly in the garden in any sunny, well-drained garden spot in dry to average soil. It thrives in gravelly sites and self-sows abundantly. Sow every two weeks from midspring to midsummer to extend bloom season.
RECOMMENDED VARIETIES: 'Persian Jewels', 15 inches, has 2½-inch double flowers in pink, white, violet, and blue. The 'Miss Jekyll' series is 18 inches tall in blue, white, and rose. 'Oxford Blue' grows 30 inches tall with double blue flowers. 'Dwarf Moody Blue' is only 6 inches tall with semidouble sky blue blooms.

'Miss Jekyll Blue' love-in-a-mist

NOLANA PARADOXA

noh-LAH-nuh pay-ruh-DOK-suh

Nolana

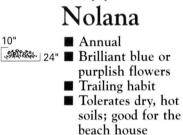

10"
24"

- Annual
- Brilliant blue or purplish flowers
- Trailing habit
- Tolerates dry, hot soils; good for the beach house

Nolana's 2-inch-wide, tubular, dark blue flowers have a contrasting white or yellow throat. They stay closed on cloudy days. This South American native, a tender perennial grown as an annual, is 4 to 10 inches high with a sprawling form.
USES: Nolana is good for edging and rock gardens, for the front of the border, and for spilling over the sides of containers and hanging baskets. It looks best with other low-growing plants such as Mexican evening primrose and sweet alyssum.
CULTURE: Nolana likes dry, sandy conditions and tolerates heat and salt. Sow in place or plant seedlings in full sun 4 to 6 inches apart; do not fertilize.
RECOMMENDED VARIETIES: 'Blue Bird', 6 inches tall, has a white throat. 'Snowbird' is 6 inches tall with all-white blossoms. 'Blue Ensign' is a darker blue. *N. napiformis* 'Sky Blue', 10 inches tall, has a blue throat. *N. humifusa* is 10 inches tall and trails 18 to 24 inches wide, with silvery blue flowers that have dark blue throats.

'Snowbird' nolana

OENOTHERA SPP.

oh-NAH-thuh-ruh

Evening primrose, sundrops

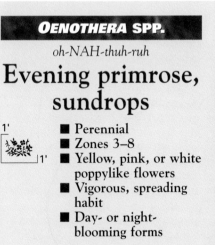

1'
1'

- Perennial
- Zones 3–8
- Yellow, pink, or white poppylike flowers
- Vigorous, spreading habit
- Day- or night-blooming forms

These hardy North American wildflowers grow from 6 inches to 2 feet tall and spread up to 2½ feet across, depending on the variety. Sundrops open in the morning and close at night, whereas evening primroses open in the afternoon and close by morning.
USES: Use in rock gardens, wildflower gardens, and massed in borders. Short ones are good edgers.
CULTURE: Provide well-drained, average soil in sun to partial shade. These plants bloom in summer and are easy to grow. Restrict their spread by pulling or digging them out by the roots or by dividing every few years. They tolerate drought, heat, and poor, dry soil.
RECOMMENDED VARIETIES: *O. fruticosa* 'Fireworks' is 1 to 2 feet high with yellow flowers. *O. speciosa* 'Rosea', Mexican evening primrose, is 1 foot tall and pink. *O. macrocarpa fremontii* 'Lemon Silver' is 6 inches tall with big, lemon flowers. *O. caespitosa*, fragrant white evening primrose, opens intensely fragrant white flowers every evening in summer. It grows 8 inches high.

'Rosea' Mexican evening primrose

ORIGANUM SPP.

oh-RIH-guh-num

Oregano

'Kent Beauty' oregano

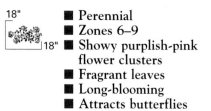

18"
18"

- Perennial
- Zones 6–9
- Showy purplish-pink flower clusters
- Fragrant leaves
- Long-blooming
- Attracts butterflies

The genus *Origanum* has many delightful, drought-tolerant cultivars that belong in the flower garden. Most grow 1 to 2 feet tall and 1½ feet wide with a somewhat sprawling, spreading habit.

USES: Grow massed as ground cover in beds and borders, as a weaver through other plants, and for cutting.

CULTURE: Plant in full sun in average, well-drained soil. Oregano cannot tolerate wet feet. It may need winter mulch to ensure survival north of Zone 6.

RECOMMENDED VARIETIES: *O. laevigatum* 'Herrenhausen' is one of the best ornamental oreganos for its abundant sprays of showy maroon flowers in summer and fall and purple fall foliage. It has a 1-foot sprawling form. 'Hopleys' is 18 inches tall and wide with lavender to deep blue flowers. A number of hybrids are also beautiful garden plants. 'Rosenkuppel' has an erect form with bright pink to mauve blossoms. 'Nymphenburg' grows 20 inches tall with pink flowers. 'Kent Beauty' has small pink flowers and large, showy, bright pink bracts.

PAEONIA HYBRIDS

pay-OH-nee-uh

Herbaceous peony

'Mons Jules Elie' peony

3'
3'

- Perennial
- Zones 3–8
- Big fragrant blooms
- Handsome leaves
- Many flower forms and colors

Lavish blooms in late spring, glossy, dark green summer leaves, and bronzy fall foliage make peonies valuable all season. They grow up to 3 feet tall with flowers up to 8 inches across. Grow early-, mid-, and late-season varieties for blooms over a month or more.

USES: Peonies make good hedges and border plants. They look lovely in beds underplanted with later-blooming annuals and perennials.

CULTURE: Peonies like full sun and well-drained soil rich in organic matter. Plant bare-root in early fall with the eyes, or buds, 2 inches below the ground. Mound old compost or rotten manure around the base in early spring, but keep it off the stems. Peonies may need staking. Set a circular peony stake over the plant when it's 1 foot high.

RECOMMENDED VARIETIES: 'Sarah Bernhardt' has double light pink flowers early. 'Mons Jules Elie' bears fragrant double rose-pink flowers in early season. 'Raspberry Sundae' has cream flowers flushed with deep pink in midseason. 'Pink Parfait' bears large, fragrant, double pink flowers in late season.

PAPAVER SPP.

pah-PAH-ver

Poppy

'Allegro' Oriental poppy

3'
2'

- Annuals and perennials
- Zones 3–7
- Intense, hot colors

Poppies add brilliant, hot colors to the late spring and early summer garden with flowers that range from 1 to 7 inches wide. They can be 6 inches to 4 feet tall.

USES: Poppies make wonderful plants for the border with attention-grabbing red or orange colors. Foliage disappears by midsummer; interplant with annuals or late-emerging perennials to hide the hole it leaves.

CULTURE: Best in full sun and average to rich, well-drained soil. Many poppies self-sow. Oriental poppies form large clumps that can be divided if they outgrow their site.

RECOMMENDED VARIETIES: *P. nudicaule* (Iceland poppy, annual): 'Meadow Pastels', 2 feet, soft pinks and creams; 'Partyfun Hybrids', 14 inches, brighter pink, yellow, orange, and scarlet. *P. somniferum* (peony-flowered poppy, annual): 'Danish Flag', 3 to 4 feet, with fringed blooms 4 to 5 inches wide in deep scarlet and white; 'Oase', 3 feet, a big double red. *P. orientale* (Oriental poppy, perennial): 'Allegro', 16 inches, red flowers with a black center; 'Fatima', white with pink edge and dark spots; 'Watermelon', deep rose. *P. rhoeas* (Shirley poppy, annual): 'Legion of Honor', red with a dark center.

PATRINIA SCABIOSIFOLIA

pah-TRIN-ee-uh
skab-ee-oh-sih-FOH-lee-uh

Golden lace

36"
40"

- Perennial
- Zones 4–8
- Airy clusters of tiny yellow flowers
- Imposing height
- Late summer to fall bloom
- Self-sows freely

Unfamiliar to many gardeners, this easy perennial is useful for its clouds of yellow flowers 3 to 6 feet above a mound of coarse leaves.

USES: Use golden lace at the back or middle of the border, where its flower stems are visible but its rather unattractive foliage is obscured. Excellent in wild gardens with tall ornamental grasses. Or plant with *Verbena bonariensis* and purple coneflower.

CULTURE: Prefers moist, well-drained, humusy soil and sun to partial shade but can tolerate some drought once established.

RECOMMENDED VARIETIES: 'Nagoya' is 2 to 3 feet tall with red fall foliage. *P. gibbosa* (Zones 5–9) has yellow blooms on 12- to 15-inch stems. *P. triloba* has yellow flowers on a 12-inch mound of leaves.

Golden lace

PELARGONIUM X HORTORUM

pel-ar-GOH-nee-um hor-TOH-rum

Geranium

18"
15"

- Tender perennial grown as an annual
- Zones 8–10
- Brilliant, hot colors
- Spring to fall bloom

Geranium's lavish blooms and pretty leaves adorn window boxes throughout the world. These tender perennials, mostly native to South Africa, vary in habit from 8-inch mounded edging plants to 18-inch-high trailers with a 2-foot spread.

Usually grown as an annual.

USES: Perfect for bedding, borders, edging, houseplants, and containers.

CULTURE: Best in full sun and moist, well-drained soil. Removing spent flowers improves the plant's appearance and encourages new blooms. Pinch stem tips to prevent legginess on mounded cultivars.

RECOMMENDED VARIETIES: Hundreds of varieties available. Some of the best bedders are 'Stardust Mix', 8 to 12 inches, star-shaped flowers in pink, red, salmon, and red and white with starry leaves; 'Tango Orange', 12 to 15 inches, intense orange on strong stems; 'Maverick Hybrids', 16 inches tall with 5- to 6-inch flower heads in shades of red, pink, violet, and bicolors; and 'Orbit Hybrids', densely branched, compact plants 14 inches tall with good leaf zoning.

Geranium 'Orbit Hybrids'

PEROVSKIA ATRIPLICIFOLIA

puh-ROV-skee-uh
at-rip-lih-sih-FOH-lee-uh

Russian sage

3'
4'

- Perennial
- Zones 2–9
- Lavender-blue flowers
- Silvery gray leaves
- Drought- and heat-tolerant

This fine-textured, bushy perennial starts blooming in late June and continues into October. It grows 3 to 4 feet tall.

USES: Makes a cloud of feathery foliage in the midborder, where its open habit gives it a casual look. Silvery Russian sage looks attractive contrasted with the reddish-purple leaves of 'Velvet Cloak' smokebush, or with a lemon yellow daylily such as 'Happy Returns'.

CULTURE: Prefers full sun and well-drained, average soil. Prune hard when new growth appears in spring.

RECOMMENDED VARIETIES: 'Filigran', 2 to 3 feet, with finely cut leaves and light blue flowers; 'Longin', 3 feet, with upright growth, narrow leaves, and violet-blue flowers; 'Blue Spire', 3 feet, with finely dissected leaves. 'Little Spire' is only 18 inches tall.

'Blue Spire' Russian sage

PETUNIA 'WAVE' SERIES

puh-TOO-nee-uh

'Wave' series petunia

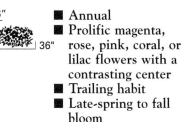

- ■ Annual
- ■ Prolific magenta, rose, pink, coral, or lilac flowers with a contrasting center
- ■ Trailing habit
- ■ Late-spring to fall bloom

'Purple Wave' petunia

A valuable ground cover or trailing container plant, this remarkable annual flowers abundantly all season, covering large areas with colorful blooms. 'Purple Wave' is only 3 to 6 inches tall and spreads or trails up to an astonishing 5 feet, with brilliant 3-inch, rosy purple blooms. Other varieties are slightly taller with a narrower spread.

USES: The 'Wave' series petunias make excellent ground covers. Their long bloom period is perfect for hanging baskets and containers.

CULTURE: Petunias prefer full sun and moist, well-drained soil rich in organic matter. They need regular watering and occasional feeding. Although many petunias require deadheading and pruning to look good, this variety grows rapidly and flowers lavishly with no extra care.

RECOMMENDED VARIETIES: There are hundreds of beautiful hybrid petunias. Other spreading types include the 'Supertunia' series, with saturated colors, and 'Surfinia' series, with veined pastel tones, a trailing habit, and fragrant flowers.

PHASEOLUS COCCINEUS

fay-zee-OH-lus kok-SIN-ee-us

Scarlet runner bean

- ■ Annual vine that twines and clings by tendrils
- ■ Bright red flowers
- ■ Delicious pods, seeds, and bean-flavored flowers
- ■ Attracts hummingbirds
- ■ Fast-growing

Scarlet runner bean

This tropical American vine climbs 15 feet and produces scarlet red flowers followed by long green edible pods that taste scrumptious when cooked.

USES: Grow on trellises, arbors, bamboo tepees, and other supports. A must for edible gardens, it also looks good trellised with climbing white roses.

CULTURE: Scarlet runner bean likes a position in full sun and moist, well-drained soil of average fertility. Seeds are large and easy to plant outdoors. Harvest pods when 4 inches long, or let them grow bigger, pick them at the end of the season, and dry the seeds.

RECOMMENDED VARIETIES: 'Painted Lady', an heirloom variety, has bicolored, cream-and-coral flowers. 'Scarlet Bees' is a heat-tolerant, 2-foot bush with scarlet flowers. 'Sunset' has salmon-pink flowers, and 'Prizewinner' has dazzling red flowers and 20-inch pods. 'Hammond's Dwarf' is an 18-inch bush bean with 7-inch pods.

PHLOX PANICULATA

FLOKS puh-nik-yew-LAH-tuh

Garden phlox

- ■ Perennial
- ■ Zones 3–8
- ■ Large flower clusters
- ■ Fragrant
- ■ Blooms summer to fall

'Harmony' garden phlox

A garden classic in pink, red, purple, or white, this United States native grows up to 3 feet tall.

USES: Plant in the middle of the border or in beds. Good companions include lilies, daylilies, purple coneflower, and 'Victoria' salvia. Phlox makes a fine cut flower.

CULTURE: Grow in full sun in rich, moist, well-drained soil high in organic matter. Powdery mildew can be a problem. Provide good air circulation to keep plants healthy, thinning plants where necessary. Water plants during times of drought and cut back unsightly stems, taking care to remove them without touching hands or diseased leaves to any other plant. Plant disease-resistant varieties.

RECOMMENDED VARIETIES: 'Katherine' has abundant pink flowers, strong stems, and high resistance to powdery mildew. 'David', 3 to 4 feet, has long-blooming, scented white flowers and good disease resistance, as does 'Bright Eyes', a pink-flowered form, 2½ to 3 feet tall, with ruby eyes. 'Shortwood' is a pink form of 'David'

PHYSOSTEGIA VIRGINIANA

fye-soh-STEE-jee-uh vur-jih-nee-AH-nuh

Obedient plant

3'
2'

- Perennial
- Zones 3–9
- Rosy pink or white flower spikes
- Spreads quickly
- Attractive in late summer

Twist individual flowers on this North American native and they'll obediently keep their new place— a boon to flower arrangers. The species, which can be invasive, blooms from mid- to late summer and grows up to 4 feet high.

USES: Spreads quickly, making a broad, handsome swath of bright color in the wild border. Suited for groups and massing, it also makes a good cut flower.

CULTURE: Obedient plant flourishes in full sun to partial shade and tolerates both wet and dry soils. Plants flop in highly fertile soil and need regular dividing to keep their spread in check. Named varieties are less invasive than the species.

RECOMMENDED VARIETIES: 'Summer Snow', 3 feet tall with white flowers, is less invasive; 'Miss Manners' is a new clump-forming introduction that is not invasive; it bears white flowers on 2-foot plants.

'Vivid' forms tight 2-foot-tall clumps with bright pink blooms; 'Variegata' has pink blooms with variegated green and white leaves.

'Vivid' obedient plant

PLATYCODON GRANDIFLORUS

plah-tee-COH-don gran-di-FLO-rus

Balloon flower

36"
24"

- Perennial
- Zones 3–8
- Balloon-shaped buds
- Cheerful blue, pink, or white flowers
- Erect habit

Ballooning buds become bell-shaped blooms beginning in early summer. Plants form 2-foot upright clumps.

USES: Balloon flower looks effective grouped in beds and borders. It blends well with most flowers, including daylilies, garden phlox, and false sunflower.

CULTURE: Easy to grow, balloon flower prefers full sun but tolerates partial shade, which is actually preferable in hot climates. It needs well-drained soil, and tall varieties may require staking. Note where you plant balloon flower; it emerges late in the spring.

RECOMMENDED VARIETIES: 'Baby Blue', 6- to 8-inch dwarf, bushy, ideal for edging or front of the border; 'Blaue Glocke', 1 to 2 feet, blue flowers; 'Fuji White', 8 inches, lime green buds open to 1½-inch white blossoms; 'Mariesii', 1 to 2 feet, dark blue flowers.

'Sentimental Blue' balloon flower

PORTULACA GRANDIFLORA

por-tew-LAH-kuh gran-di-FLO-ruh

Moss rose

6"
12"

- Annual
- Bright blooms close on gray days
- Forms a trailing mat
- Tolerates heat, drought, and lean soil

This Brazilian native thrives in hot, dry weather and poor soil, creating a carpet of brilliant 1-inch flowers with small, succulent foliage.

USES: Moss rose is excellent in containers and hanging baskets. It forms a mass of mixed colors in rock gardens and on dry slopes and makes an effective ground cover where bright color is desired. It also works well in paving cracks and other dry areas. Grow it with verbena, gazania, and 'Thai Silk' California poppies.

CULTURE: Grow moss rose in dry, well-drained soil in hot, full sun.

RECOMMENDED VARIETIES: 'Afternoon Delight', 6 inches, double 1½-inch flowers, brilliant shades of white, yellow, red, orange, and pink, stays open later; 'Sundial Hybrids', 4 inches, including peach, cream, orange, white, fuchsia, mango, scarlet, pink, yellow, and peppermint (pink with crimson marks); 'Cloud Beater' stays open all day. 'Yubi Hybrids' have bright colors and succulent, gray, trailing foliage good for containers.

'Yubi Yellow' moss rose

POTENTILLA SPP.

poh-ten-TIL-luh

Cinquefoil

'Primrose Beauty' bush cinquefoil

- Deciduous shrub
- Zones 2–9
- Yellow, orange, salmon, red, pink, or white flowers
- Shrubby and herbaceous forms
- Exceptionally hardy

Many forms of this versatile genus bloom from June to September. Low-growing plants, shrubby potentillas grow up to 36 inches tall and wide; herbaceous varieties grow 4 to 12 inches high.

USES: Cinquefoil is an excellent choice for low-maintenance, dry gardens. Plant it in rockeries, as edging for the perennial border, or in seaside gardens. Use shrubs as a ground cover or foundation plant.

CULTURE: Cinquefoil prefers full sun and fertile, well-drained soil but tolerates partial shade, poor soil, salt, and severe cold.

RECOMMENDED VARIETIES: *P. fruticosa* (bush cinquefoil): 'Abbotswood', irregular, mounding habit, 3 feet high and wide, white; 'Primrose Beauty', 3 feet, primrose yellow flowers with a dark center and gray-green leaves. Herbaceous forms inclue *P. nepalensis* (Nepal cinquefoil): 'Miss Willmott', 1-foot sprawling habit with rosy red flowers, and *P. megalantha* (wooly cinquefoil): 1 foot, clustered golden flowers with attractive green leaves.

RHODODENDRON SPP.

roh-doh-DEN-drun

Rhododendron, azalea

'PJM Victor' rhododendron

- Evergreen or deciduous shrub
- Zones 4–10, depending on variety
- Beautiful spring or summer flowers

The 900 species of this genus include both deciduous and evergreen rhododendrons and azaleas. Plants are rounded and vary from miniatures several inches high to species 20 feet high.

USES: Plant at the foundation, in woodland gardens, in shrub or mixed borders, and in wild gardens.

CULTURE: Grow in well-drained, acid soil with ample organic matter. Plants in northern gardens need less shade than those in the South. Keep away from salt, alkaline soil, and locations exposed to winter's intense sunlight and severe wind.

RECOMMENDED VARIETIES: Thousands of cultivars and species are available. Some of the hardiest evergreen rhododendrons are *R. catawbiense* (catawba rhododendron, Zones 4–7), with reddish-purple flowers ('Album' has white flowers); *R. maximum* (rosebay rhododendron, Zones 4–7), with white or rosy purple blooms; 'PJM' hybrids (Zones 5–8), with pink to purple flowers; and the old ironclad 'Boule de Neige' (Zones 4–7), with white flowers. Hardiest evergreen azaleas include the Shammarello hybrids (Zones 5–9).

ROSA HYBRIDS

ROH-zuh

Rose

'Bonica' shrub rose

- Deciduous shrub
- Zones 4–10, depending on variety
- Lavish flowers
- Many are fragrant

Roses have a reputation for being hard to grow without a regimen of fungicides, insecticides, and pruning. Some, however, require little care and provide more than one season of garden interest.

USES: Select everblooming varieties for all-summer color. Grow climbers on trellises and arbors. Use low-growing types and miniatures as ground covers. Many modern shrub roses work well in informal mixed or shrub borders.

CULTURE: Plant in sun and well-drained, fertile, slightly acid soil rich with compost. Prune to remove dead stems and keep in bounds.

RECOMMENDED VARIETIES: Still the best landscape rose is 'The Fairy', a disease-free polyantha with pink blossoms all summer. Other easy shrubs include the Meidilland series; 'Bonica' is pink. Best modern shrubs include the 'Romantica' series: 'Frederic Mistral' is glowing pink. 'Mary Marshall' is an easy pink miniature. Top ground covers are the Flower Carpet series. 'New Dawn' is a vigorous, hardy climber with pale pink flowers all summer. 'Climbing Iceberg' has fragrant white blooms all summer.

RUDBECKIA SPP.

rud-BEK-ee-uh

Black-eyed Susan

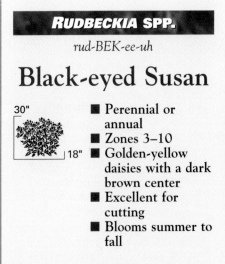

30"
18"

- Perennial or annual
- Zones 3–10
- Golden-yellow daisies with a dark brown center
- Excellent for cutting
- Blooms summer to fall

Growers have developed many attractive selections of this North American wildflower, ranging from 1 to 8 feet tall. Rays can be single or double in gold or lemon yellow; the centers vary from dark brown to purplish-brown or green.

USES: Grow in late-summer beds and borders, in meadow and prairie gardens, and for bouquets. Seed heads provide winter interest.

CULTURE: Plant in rich, moist, well-drained soil. Black-eyed Susan may self-sow in favorable conditions and spreads by rhizomes. Most types are somewhat drought-tolerant, including gloriosa daisy and 'Goldsturm' black-eyed Susan, although both perform best in moist conditions.

RECOMMENDED VARIETIES:
R. hirta (gloriosa daisy) cultivars are best grown as annuals. Good varieties include 'Indian Summer', 3 to 4 feet, golden-orange daisies, drought-tolerant; 'Irish Eyes', 2½ feet, yellow flowers with green eyes; 'Goldilocks', with double golden-orange flowers on 2-foot plants; 'Sonora', a low-growing (16-inch) plant with clear yellow flowers; and 'Rustic Colors', 1½ feet, orange, bronze, and bicolors. *R. fulgida* 'Goldsturm' is a classic perennial that reaches 2 to 3 feet high with neon-gold rays and dark brown disks. It is hardy in Zones 4–9. 'Herbstonne' grows 5 to 7 feet high with large, drooping, lemon yellow daisies. It is very attractive to butterflies, and moisture-tolerant.

'Goldsturm' black-eyed Susan

'Rustic Colors' gloriosa daisy

SALVIA SPP.

SAL-vee-uh

Sage; salvia

18"
10"

- Annual or perennial
- Zones 3–8, depending on variety
- Red, blue, violet, pink, and white flowers
- Attracts butterflies and hummingbirds

Salvia's flower spikes stay colorful long after blooming, thanks to the decorative bracts that remain.

USES: Salvia looks terrific massed in beds and borders. It's good for edging, container planting, and cutting. It grows from 1 to 5 feet tall, depending on the variety.

CULTURE: Salvia prefers well-drained soil of average fertility and full sun to light shade. Some varieties tolerate heat and drought.

RECOMMENDED VARIETIES:
S. officinalis, culinary sage, Zones 4–9, has attractive, aromatic gray-green leaves and lavender flowers. *S. verticillata* 'Purple Rain', 1 to 2 feet, Zones 4–7, is a perennial with constantly blooming purple flowers on long stems. Excellent hardy hybrids (*S. × sylvestris*, Zones 3–9) include 'May Night', 1 to 2 feet, with dark violet-blue spikes; 'Blue Hill', 1 to 2 feet, clear blue; and 'East Friesland', 2 to 3 feet, violet. *S. chamaedryoides* (germander sage, Zones 8–10) is a drought-tolerant ground cover for gardens in the West, with bright blue flowers and silvery leaves on low, 6-inch, spreading plants. *S. splendens* 'Hotline Hybrids', 10 to 12 inches, is a popular annual in red, white, burgundy, salmon, violet, and purple with blue and white streaks. *S. farinacea* 'Victoria', 18 inches, bears long-lasting violet-blue spikes. It can be grown as an annual. *S. coccinea*, Texas sage, is a tender perennial grown as an annual that reaches 2 feet high with delicate, open flower spikes. 'Snow Nymph' is white; 'Coral Nymph' is a coral-and-white bicolor; 'Lady in Red', 12 to 15 inches, is scarlet. *S. sclarea*, clary sage, 2 to 5 feet, has bicolored blooms in white, pink, and lilac.

'Bonfire' annual salvia (S. splendens)

'May Night' salvia (S. × sylvestris)

SANVITALIA PROCUMBENS

san-vih-TAL-ee-uh pro-KUM-benz

Creeping zinnia

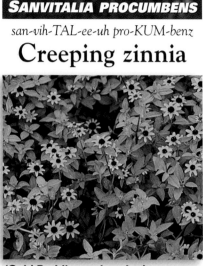

'Gold Braid' creeping zinnia

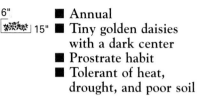

6"
15"

- ■ Annual
- ■ Tiny golden daisies with a dark center
- ■ Prostrate habit
- ■ Tolerant of heat, drought, and poor soil

Creeping zinnia blankets the ground from June to frost with charming, dark-eyed, golden daisies against a background of pointed green leaves. An annual, this native of Mexico grows 6 inches tall.

USES: Use creeping zinnia massed for a summer ground cover; as a uniform edging, in beds, borders, containers, hanging baskets, and rock gardens; and in crevices between pavers and stone walls.

Complementary companions are white sweet alyssum, flossflower, and multicolored moss rose.

CULTURE: Creeping zinnia requires no special watering or feeding. It thrives in full sun and light, well-drained soil but tolerates some shade and other soils.

RECOMMENDED VARIETIES: 'Mandarin Orange' grows 8 inches high with a 12- to 16-inch spread and ½-inch orange blooms; 'Mandarin Yellow' has lemon yellow flowers. 'Yellow Carpet' grows 4 to 6 inches high. The single flowers are lemon yellow with black centers. 'Gold Braid' grows 4 inches high with single golden-yellow blossoms.

SAPONARIA SPP.

sap-oh-NAY-ree-uh

Soapwort

Soapwort (S. ocymoides)

6"
24"

- ■ Perennial
- ■ Zones 3–8, depending on species
- ■ Abundant pink flowers
- ■ Spreading, trailing habit

This perennial forms a sprawling cushion of rosy pink flowers. It ranges from 6 inches to 2 feet high, depending on the species.

USES: Soapwort looks wonderful draped over the edges of stone walls, in rock gardens, and in naturalized borders and beds. Its trailing stems also weave effectively through other plants for an informal look.

CULTURE: Soapwort thrives in

moist, well-drained soils in full sun to part shade. It can spread vigorously, but the excess can be pulled out easily by the roots. Cut back *S. ocymoides* after blooming to keep it from looking stringy. Pinch *S. officinalis* in spring for fuller growth.

RECOMMENDED VARIETIES: *S. lempergii* 'Max Frei' (Zones 5–7) is 1 foot tall with light pink flowers in June and July. It is drought-tolerant. *S. ocymoides* is 1 foot tall with rosy flowers in May and June, good for dry, sunny banks in Zones 3–8; *S. officinalis* 'Rosea Plena' (Zones 2–8) has scented, pale-pink double flowers from June through September on an upright, spreading mound.

SCABIOSA COLUMBARIA 'BUTTERFLY BLUE' AND 'PINK MIST'

skay-bee-OH-suh kol-lum-BAR-ee-uh

Pincushion flower

'Butterfly Blue' pincushion flower

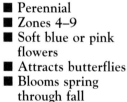

12"
18"

- ■ Perennial
- ■ Zones 4–9
- ■ Soft blue or pink flowers
- ■ Attracts butterflies
- ■ Blooms spring through fall

These delightful perennials bring long-lasting pastel color to the garden and an unending supply of blooms for cutting. The frilly pincushions top 12-inch stems that emerge from a low gray-green mound of basal leaves.

USES: Pincushion flower works well massed in beds, at the front of a border, in rock gardens, and in cottage gardens. In northern

climates, it can bring a touch of color to the garden through Thanksgiving. Grow with 'Bath's Pink' dianthus or 'Lulu' and 'Tangerine Gem' signet marigolds.

CULTURE: Plant in full sun and well-drained soil. Mulch and water during times of drought. Clip the finely bristled green seed heads and add them to fresh arrangements; deadheading will prolong bloom. Do not cut back in fall.

RECOMMENDED VARIETIES: *S. caucasica* 'Perfecta Alba', 2 to 3 feet, has large white flowers that bloom June to September, Zones 3–7; 'Perfecta' is lavender-blue. 'Fama', 18 inches tall, has lavender-blue flowers with silver centers.

SEDUM 'AUTUMN JOY'

SEE-dum

'Autumn Joy' sedum

24"
18"

- Perennial
- Zones 3–9
- Light green flowers in early summer turn pink in late summer, russet in fall and winter
- Attracts butterflies

Truly one of the great garden plants, 'Autumn Joy' sedum brings color and structure to the garden in summer, fall, and winter. It forms clumps 18 to 36 inches tall and wide that hold their form all winter and make a stunning contrast to ornamental grasses.

USES: Consider using it in beds, borders, foundations, and rock gardens. Place it where you'll see it year-round.

CULTURE: Plant in full sun and well-drained soil, preferably high in organic matter. For tighter clumps, divide in spring. Pinch back stem tips in early spring for shorter, more floriferous plants.

RECOMMENDED VARIETIES: *S. spectabile* 'Brilliant' is similar but bears garish hot-pink flowers in August. It is smaller and does not hold its form through winter as well as 'Autumn Joy'. 'Vera Jameson', 10 to 12 inches tall, has dusky pink flowers and mahogany leaves.

'Autumn Joy' sedum in early fall

SPIRAEA JAPONICA 'ANTHONY WATERER'

spy-REE-uh jah-PAW-nih-kah

'Anthony Waterer' Japanese spirea

3'
4'

- Deciduous shrub
- Zones 4–8
- Dark pink flowers
- Mounded habit
- Red fall color

This deciduous shrub starts blooming in early June and continues on and off until fall. Flowers are deep rose, and new leaves are reddish-bronze, turning rich green, then red in fall. It matures to 4 feet high and wide.

USES: Use for low, informal hedges and in shrub or mixed borders for its long-lasting blooms. It tends to spread with age and makes a good, tall, shrubby ground cover in front of other shrubs, bringing variety to foundation plantings.

CULTURE: Grow in well-drained soil in full sun to partial shade. Prune by half in early spring or renew by cutting to the ground. You can also cut it back after the first flush of bloom to stimulate fresh bronze leaves and August rebloom.

RECOMMENDED VARIETIES: 'Goldflame', 2 to 3 feet, has rosy flowers with golden-chartreuse leaves in summer and red, copper, and orange leaves in spring and fall; 'Shibori' is a 3-foot mound of pink, rose, and white flowers all summer.

'Anthony Waterer' Japanese spirea

STOKESIA LAEVIS

stoh-KEE-zee-uh LAY-viss

Stokes' aster

18"
18"

- Perennial
- Zones 5–9
- Fluffy-eyed daisies with ragged petals in blue, lavender, or white
- Attracts butterflies
- Good for cutting

These showy flowers bloom all summer on 12- to 24-inch plants. Native to the South, Stokes' aster has leathery basal foliage and blooms that resemble bachelor's button and attract butterflies to the garden.

USES: Use Stokes' aster massed at the front of the border for long-lasting color. It makes a good cut flower and combines well in the garden with 'Goldsturm' or 'Goldquelle' black-eyed Susans.

CULTURE: Grow Stokes' aster in well-drained soil and full sun in the North or in partial shade in the South. Deadhead to prolong bloom season, and divide when clumps are crowded. Mulch in the North.

RECOMMENDED VARIETIES: 'Alba' has white flowers; 'Blue Danube' has blue 4-inch blooms. 'Klaus Jelitto' has lavender flowers, the largest of all cultivars; 'Silver Moon' bears silvery white flowers; 'Wyoming' is the deepest blue.

'Blue Danube' Stokes' aster

tah-GEE-teez

Marigold

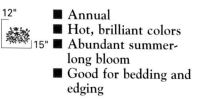

12"
15"

- Annual
- Hot, brilliant colors
- Abundant summer-long bloom
- Good for bedding and edging

'Primrose Lady' African marigold

'Granada' French marigold

Signet marigold

These versatile plants attract butterflies and bring long-lasting, bright color to your garden. Flowers, which measure from 1 inch to 5 inches across, are single or double in shades of yellow and orange, and some have red or brown markings. Easy to grow, these Mexican natives vary in height from 6-inch dwarfs to bushy plants 3 feet tall.

USES: Marigolds are excellent for bedding and edging. Plant them under taller annuals and perennials to hide leggy stems, or use them to fill visual holes left by spent perennials in the flower border. Use them in containers, kitchen gardens, and herb gardens.

CULTURE: Marigolds prefer moist, well-drained soil but tolerate many other soil types. Sow seed of tall African marigolds indoors six to eight weeks before the last frost, covering with a sprinkling of seed-starting mix, or start small varieties outdoors in late spring. Plant seedlings outdoors after the last frost. Water during drought, and deadhead for maximum bloom. Tall varieties may need staking.

RECOMMENDED VARIETIES: African marigold, *T. erecta*, is 1 to 3 feet tall with double, zinnialike heads; heat-resistant 'Inca Hybrids' are 14 inches tall and have 4- to 5-inch blooms in yellow, orange, or gold; 'French Vanilla' has creamy white, 3-inch flowers on 20-inch plants; 'Gold Coins' has 5-inch, nearly spherical, frilly blooms on 30-inch stems in yellow, orange, and gold. It makes an excellent cut flower. French marigold, *T. patula*, is 6 to 8 inches high with single or double flowers; 'Bonanza Bolero' has crested blossoms bicolored in red and yellow on 10-inch plants. Signet marigold, *T. tenuifolia*, is 12 to 24 inches tall and edible, with dainty, single flowers and ferny, aromatic leaves. Mexican mint marigold, *T. lucida*, is edible and grows up to 3 feet high and wide with single yellow flowers and licorice-scented leaves. Do not use chemicals on flowers grown for eating.

thuh-LIK-trum

Meadow rue

3'
2'

- Perennial
- Zones 4–9
- Pink, lavender, and white blooms
- Attractive, delicate leaves
- Airy habit

These graceful plants can grow 5 feet high, although most rues are about 3 feet tall and half as wide. Long stems rise from an open, layered mound of ferny foliage. Clustered blooms contain many tiny flowers for a fuzzy or frothy effect.

USES: Meadow rue looks lovely massed in beds and borders, or in woodland gardens. Tall varieties are excellent at the back of the border.

Columbine meadow rue

CULTURE: Grow in sun to partial shade in well-drained, moist soil rich in organic matter. Too much fertilizer causes plants to flop.

RECOMMENDED VARIETIES: Columbine meadow rue, *T. aquilegiifolium*, grows 2 to 3 feet high with ferny leaves similar to columbine and bright lilac, fuzzy flowers in early summer. 'Thunder Cloud' has purple flowers. Lavender mist, *T. rochebrunianum*, is 4 to 6 feet tall with blue-green leaves and deep lavender flowers in mid- to late summer. *T. delavayi* 'Hewitt's Double' bears open sprays of tiny, bright lavender pompons on 4-foot plants from midsummer to fall. 'Album' has white flowers.

THUNBERGIA ALATA

thun-BER-jee-uh ah-LAY-tuh

Black-eyed Susan vine

- Annual, twining vine
- Cheerful golden flowers with dark brown center
- Small size
- Summer to fall bloom

The stems of black-eyed Susan vine grow quickly to 6 feet long. A tender perennial treated as an annual, it is easy to grow from seed and is available in orange, yellow, and white.

USES: Grow this small vine on a trellis to bring warm color to a wall or enclosure, or on a bamboo tripod to add vertical interest in the center of a bed or border. Because it is relatively short, you can also use it as a ground cover or in containers. For a whimsical effect, plant different colors together on a tripod, or contrast it with 'Blue Bird' nolana to make a dramatic hanging basket.

CULTURE: Plant 12 inches apart in full sun to partial shade in warm, moist, fertile soil. Potted plants can be overwintered indoors.

RECOMMENDED VARIETIES: 'Suzie Hybrids' are yellow, orange, and white. 'Alba' and 'Bakeri' are white. 'Aurantiaca' has yellow-orange flowers. *T. fragrans* 'Angel Wings' has fragrant white flowers. *T. grandiflora* has blue flowers with yellow centers and leaves up to 8 inches long. It needs partial shade.

'Suzie Yellow' black-eyed Susan vine

TITHONIA ROTUNDIFOLIA

tih-THOH-nee-uh roh-tun-dih-FOH-lee-uh

Mexican sunflower

- Annual
- Bold orange daisy
- Attracts butterflies, songbirds, and hummingbirds
- Tolerates heat, humidity, and drought

This stunning plant, a native of Mexico, grows 4 to 6 feet tall and produces masses of 3-inch, blazing orange blooms from midsummer through fall.

USES: Whether you use this plant at the back of the border or as a garden specimen, it's bound to attract attention. Grow it in a sunny wildlife garden to lure hummingbirds and butterflies. It's excellent for screening unwanted views, especially when combined with tall plants such as sunflowers.

CULTURE: This plant needs sun and well-drained soil. Water during drought and stake when necessary.

RECOMMENDED VARIETIES: 'Fiesta del Sol', the best dwarf, is only 28 to 30 inches tall with 3-inch orange blooms. It is deer- and heat-resistant. 'Aztec Sun' is 4 feet tall with 3-inch golden-yellow flowers. 'Torch' is 6 feet, scarlet-orange. 'Goldfinger', 4 feet, is brilliant red-orange. 'Sundance', 3 feet, is scarlet-orange.

'Goldfinger' Mexican sunflower

TRADESCANTIA SPP.

tra-des-KAN-tee-uh

Spiderwort

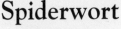

- Perennial
- Zones 3–9
- Flowers in shades of purple, blue, pink, and white
- Spreading clump of grasslike leaves
- Blooms spring to fall

This foolproof perennial produces abundant, three-petaled, showy flowers in a variety of colors. It grows about 2 feet tall and wide.

USES: Good at the front of the border, spilling over the side of a woodland path, and in moist areas. Plant it with rose mallow, obedient plant, Japanese iris, and columbine for attractive textural contrast.

CULTURE: Prefers full sun to partial shade and moist, well-drained soil. After its first bloom in late spring, cut the plant back to the ground for fresh leaves, more flowers, and a tighter form. Make sure it has plenty of moisture, particularly in sunny locations.

RECOMMENDED VARIETIES: 'Caerulea Plena', double light blue; 'Isis', rich blue; 'Concord Grape', intense purple flowers with blue-green foliage and excellent repeat bloom; 'Purple Dome', dark purple; 'Hawaiian Punch', big magenta blooms; 'Osprey', white with a magenta-pink center.

Spiderwort

TROPAEOLUM MAJUS

troh-pee-OH-lum MAY-jus

Nasturtium

'Princess of India' nasturtium

1' — 5'

- Annual
- Bright flowers in fiery tones
- Green, blue-green, or variegated leaves
- Trailing or mounded varieties
- Edible seeds, flowers, and leaves

The flowers of this delightful annual come in hot colors with a flaring trumpet shape attractive to nectar-hungry hummingbirds.

USES: Grow trailing types as a luxuriant ground cover cascading over fences and walls or clambering up netting as a screen. Mounding forms make a charming edging, and both types work well in containers, window boxes, and hanging baskets.

CULTURE: Plant seed directly in the garden in full sun to part shade after the last frost. Nasturtium likes average to poor, moist, well-drained soil. Too much fertilizer can reduce flowering. Plants prefer cool-summer climates and cease blooming in extreme heat.

RECOMMENDED VARIETIES: 'Jewel of Africa', 4- to 5-foot stems, peach, yellow, red, and cream flowers with variegated leaves; 'Moonlight', 7-foot vine with light yellow flowers; 'Empress of India', 12-inch mound, scarlet flowers, dark foliage; 'Alaska Hybrids', 12- to 15-inch mound, variegated leaves, pastel flowers.

TULIPA HYBRIDS

TOO-lip-uh

Tulip

'Ad Rem' tulip

15" — 6"

- Perennial bulb
- Zones 4–8, depending on variety
- Rainbow of colors
- Spring-blooming

These easy-to-grow bulbs are emblems of spring. By planting early-, mid-, and late-blooming varieties, you can enjoy tulips from early spring almost to early summer.

USES: Massed tulips make terrific bedding displays, and are lovely in containers. Force tulip bulbs indoors as a harbinger of spring.

CULTURE: Grow in full sun in well-drained soil. Plant bulbs up to 12 inches deep and 8 inches apart, and water during a dry spring but not during dry summers. View tulips as annuals in warm climates, but in cold climates tulips, especially species tulips, are perennial.

RECOMMENDED VARIETIES: Hundreds of varieties are available. *T. tarda* is an early-blooming species 4 to 6 inches tall, with white starry flowers that are yellow inside. The Darwin hybrids are 20 to 24 inches tall with big single flowers in many colors in mid- to late spring. *T. greigii* 'Plaisir' is 6 to 8 inches tall with rose-pink petals edged in cream in mid- to late spring. Its attractive foliage is dark purple striped with gray. 'Angelique' is a popular, pink, peony-flowered tulip for late season. 'Mount Tacoma' is similar in white.

VERBASCUM SPP.

ver-BASS-kum

Mullein

Purple mullein (V. phoeniceum)

3' — 2'

- Perennial or biennal
- Zones 3–8
- Tall flower spikes
- Big, hairy, gray-green basal leaves
- Architectural form

Most garden-worthy mulleins are biennials or short-lived perennials with tall stalks of yellow, white, copper, purple, and bicolored flowers arising from rosettes of woolly leaves. These drought-tolerant plants grow from 3 to 6 feet high.

USES: Excellent for adding vertical interest to beds, borders, containers, and wildflower gardens. Use with rounded or flat-topped spreading forms for maximum contrast.

CULTURE: Plant in well-drained soil in full sun to partial shade. Deadheading encourages side branching and more flowers. Although most are not long-lived, they self-sow in good conditions. Heat- and drought-tolerant.

RECOMMENDED VARIETIES: *V. chaixii album*, 3 feet, has fuzzy gray-green leaves and magenta-centered white flowers from late spring through summer. Turkish mullein, *V. bombyciferum* 'Polarsommer', produces 6-foot butter yellow flower spikes and silver leaves; 'Silver Lining' has cooler yellow flowers. Purple mullein, *V. phoeniceum*, has violet-pink flowers on 4-foot stalks with green leaves.

VERBENA SPP.

ver-BEE-nuh

Verbena

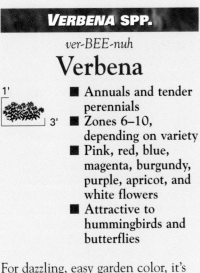

1'
3'

- Annuals and tender perennials
- Zones 6–10, depending on variety
- Pink, red, blue, magenta, burgundy, purple, apricot, and white flowers
- Attractive to hummingbirds and butterflies

For dazzling, easy garden color, it's hard to beat verbena. From ground cover varieties 6 inches tall to the versatile, 4-foot-tall *V. bonariensis*, this plant holds its own among sun-loving garden flowers.

USES: Grow in containers, hanging baskets, and window boxes, and massed in beds, borders, and rock gardens. Some short varieties of *V. × hybrida* make good ground covers in sun. *V. bonariensis* is lovely massed in the middle of the border or weaving in and out of other plants. It is also good for cutting.

CULTURE: Plant in full sun and well-drained, light, fertile soil. It benefits from regular feeding and moderate watering. Keep away from damp areas, where it may suffer from mildew. Can tolerate drought and poor to average soils.

RECOMMENDED VARIETIES: *V. bonariensis* (Zones 6–10) has purple flower clusters on airy 4-foot stems for four months. Native *V. canadensis* (Zones 7–9) 'Homestead Purple' grows 12 to 15 inches high and 3 feet wide with big purple flower heads that bloom from June to November. *V. tenuisecta* 'Tapien Blue' grows 12 inches tall with lavender-blue flower clusters, good mildew resistance, and a vigorous, spreading habit. *V. × hybrida* 'Peaches and Cream' is 8 inches tall and 24 inches wide with peachy cream flowers; 'Quartz Burgundy' is 12 inches high with deep red flowers. It is vigorous and mildew-resistant.

'Homestead Purple' verbena

'Tapien Lavender' verbena

VIOLA SPP. AND HYBRIDS

VYE-oh-luh

Violet, pansy, viola

8"
12"

- Annuals and hardy perennials
- Zones 4–9
- Old-fashioned flowers in nearly every color imaginable, including bicolors and tricolors
- Spring- and fall-blooming
- Best in cool climates

Pansies (*V. × wittrockiana*) are the largest-flowered and least hardy of this group. Violas (*V. cornuta* hybrids) have smaller flowers (up to 1½ inches wide) and are hardier; the truly perennial species violets have the smallest flowers (usually ½-inch wide or less) of the three.

USES: These make lovely additions to woodland gardens as an edging or ground cover. You can also use them in late winter or early spring along pathways, in rock gardens and beds, and in window boxes or other containers. Pansies are favorite bedding annuals for cool-season color in fall and spring. They decline as summer grows warm. In mild-winter climates, some pansies can bloom from autumn to spring.

CULTURE: Grow in full sun to partial shade in well-drained, fertile soil. Sow seed in fall, or space seedlings 12 inches apart in spring.

RECOMMENDED VARIETIES: Worthy cultivars of pansy (*V. × wittrockiana*) are many. Look for heat- as well as cold-tolerant varieties such as 'Crystal Bowl Hybrids'. 'Antique Shades' is a pastel blend with smoky, dark tones like stained glass. Violas (*V. cornuta* hybrids) are nearly as numerous as pansies. Try 'Black Magic', a long-blooming, near-black viola with a tiny yellow eye, hardy in Zones 4–9. 'Yesterday, Today, & Tomorrow', from the 'Sorbet' series of violas, opens white, then deepens to lavender-blue. *V. odorata*, sweet violet, grows 6 to 8 inches tall and 12 inches wide. It is an old-fashioned favorite for its fragrant flowers in rose, white, or violet.

'Belmont Blue' viola

'Delta Purple Rose' pansy

VITEX AGNUS-CASTUS

VYE-teks AG-nus-KAS-tus

Chaste tree

Chaste tree

20' / 20'

- Deciduous large shrub or small tree
- Zones 6–9
- Loose, pointed clusters of fragrant, light purple flowers
- Rounded form with open branches
- Good seaside plant

Not only does chaste tree have fragrant blooms up to 6 inches long from late June through September, it also has pungent-scented gray-green leaves. A native of southern Europe and western Asia, it grows 8 to 10 feet high.

USES: Good for shrub, mixed, and perennial borders, especially in droughty seaside locations. It combines nicely with lavender, rose of Sharon, shrub roses, and butterfly bush.

CULTURE: Plant in full sun and moist, well-drained, somewhat sandy soil. Like butterfly bush, it blooms on new wood and can be used as a perennial. Prune it a foot or so from the ground in the spring so its branching structure remains.

RECOMMENDED VARIETIES: 'Alba' has white flowers; 'Blushing Spires' blooms in pale pink; the flowers of 'Abbeville Blue' are dark blue; 'Montrose Purple' has violet blooms on vigorous plants.

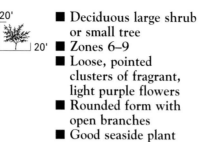

ZINNIA SPP.

ZIN-nee-uh

Zinnia

'Scarlet Ruffles' zinnia

'Peter Pan Gold' zinnia

24" / 8"

- Annual
- Brilliant flowers on bushy plants
- Attracts songbirds, hummingbirds, and butterflies
- Good cut flowers
- Forms can be upright, bushy, or spreading

Native to Mexico, zinnias are easy to grow, and they bloom for months in an array of bright warm colors and bicolors, including fire-engine red, clear pink, white, yellow, and orange. Petals can be single, double, or ruffled. Flowers are 2 to 6 inches wide on stems 4 to 40 inches tall, depending on the variety.

USES: Plant in beds, borders, containers, and cutting gardens. It's a good filler when planted near spent border perennials. Short varieties make good edgers. Plant in masses for striking color effects, or in smaller groups for color accents.

'Orange Star' Mexican zinnia (Z. haageana)

CULTURE: Grow zinnias in average, well-drained soil in full sun. They thrive in hot, dry conditions. Avoid wetting leaves when watering, because mildew can be a problem. Deadhead and fertilize lightly for maximum bloom.

RECOMMENDED VARIETIES: For low-maintenance, mildew-free bedding, plant Z. *haageana* cultivars and hybrids (Mexican zinnia), such as the hybrid 'Pinwheel' series, 12 inches tall with 2-inch flowers; Z. *haageana* 'Crystal White'; and Z. *haageana* 'Orange Star', 9 to 12 inches high, with orange single flowers. All tolerate heat, humidity, and drought. Z. *elegans* 'Ruffles' series grows 24 inches tall and has ruffled double 3-inch blooms; 'Dreamland Hybrids' is a uniform 10 to 12 inches tall with dahlialike, 4-inch flowers in apricot, coral, pink, rose, ivory, and more; 'Peter Pan Hybrids' is another good dwarf bedding series, about 12 inches tall. 'Envy' is a popular new color for zinnias, with pale chartreuse flowers on 30-inch plants. 'Cactus Jewels Hybrids' grows 36 inches tall with frilly 4- to 5-inch, double or semidouble blooms in peach, orange, salmon, magenta, shell pink, and more. Z. *peruviana* 'Bonita Mix' produces neat, tight, 24-inch bushes covered with 1½-inch, yellow ochre and brick red single flowers with dark centers.

MAIL-ORDER SOURCES

PLANTS

André Viette Farm & Nursery
P.O. Box 1109
Fishersville, VA 22939
540-943-2315
Perennials, grasses

Bluestone Perennials
7211 Middle Ridge Road
Madison, OH 44057-3096
800-852-5243
Perennials, grasses, flowering shrubs

Brent and Becky's Bulbs
7463 Heath Trail
Gloucester, VA 23061
877-661-2852
Wide variety of bulbs

Carroll Gardens
444 East Main Street
Westminster, MD 21157
800-638-6334
Shrubs, perennials

Heirloom Old Garden Roses
24062 NE Riverside Drive
St. Paul, OR 97137
503-538-1576
Old garden, landscape, and miniature roses

Heronswood Nursery Ltd.
7530 NE 288th Street
Kingston, WA 98346
360-297-4172
Rare and unusual plants

Kurt Bluemel Inc.
2740 Greene Lane
Baldwin, MD 21013-9523
800-248-7584
Grasses, perennials

Niche Gardens
1111 Dawson Road
Chapel Hill, NC 27516
919-967-0078
Perennials, shrubs, and trees

Stokes Tropicals
P.O. Box 9868
New Iberia, LA 70562-9868
800-624-9706
Exotic plants

Wayside Gardens
1 Garden Lane
Hodges, SC 29695-0001
800-845-1124
Shrubs, perennials, tropicals, bulbs, grasses

White Flower Farm
Route 63
P.O. Box 50
Litchfield, CT 06759
800-475-0148
Perennials, shrubs, vines, bulbs, and annuals

SEED

Burpee
300 Park Avenue
Warminster, PA 18974
800-888-1447
Annual and perennial seeds, plants, shrubs

Johnny's Selected Seeds
1 Foss Hill Road
Albion, ME 04910-9731
207-437-9294
Flower and vegetable seeds

Park Seed
1 Parkton Avenue
Greenwood, SC 29647-0001
800-845-3369
Vegetable and flower seeds, bulbs, plants

Seeds of Change
P.O. Box 15700
Santa Fe, NM 87506-5700
888-762-7333
Organic flower and vegetable seeds

Shepherd's Garden Seeds
30 Irene Street
Torrington, CT 06790-6658
860-482-3638
Flower, herb, and vegetable seeds

Thompson & Morgan
220 Faraday Avenue
P.O. Box 1308
Jackson, NJ 08527-0308
800-274-7333
Flower and vegetable seeds

THE USDA PLANT HARDINESS ZONE MAP OF NORTH AMERICA

Plants are classified according to the amount of cold weather they can handle. For example, a plant listed as hardy to zone 6 will survive a winter in which the temperature drops to minus 10° F.

Warm weather also influences whether a plant will survive in your region. Although this map does not address heat hardiness, in general, if a range of hardiness zones are listed for a plant, the plant will survive winter in the coldest zone as well as tolerate the heat of the warmest zone.

To use this map, find the location of your community, then match the color band marking that area to the zone key at left.

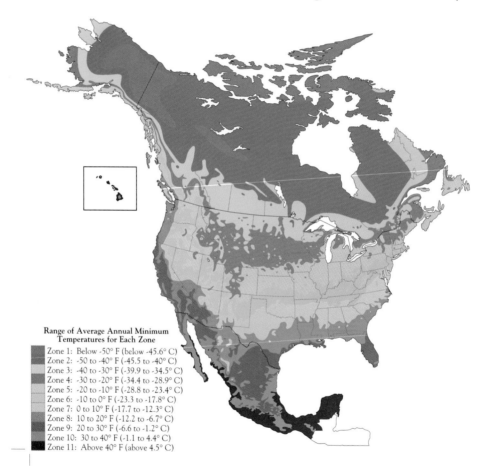

Range of Average Annual Minimum Temperatures for Each Zone

Zone 1: Below -50° F (below -45.6° C)
Zone 2: -50 to -40° F (-45.5 to -40° C)
Zone 3: -40 to -30° F (-39.9 to -34.5° C)
Zone 4: -30 to -20° F (-34.4 to -28.9° C)
Zone 5: -20 to -10° F (-28.8 to -23.4° C)
Zone 6: -10 to 0° F (-23.3 to -17.8° C)
Zone 7: 0 to 10° F (-17.7 to -12.3° C)
Zone 8: 10 to 20° F (-12.2 to -6.7° C)
Zone 9: 20 to 30° F (-6.6 to -1.2° C)
Zone 10: 30 to 40° F (-1.1 to 4.4° C)
Zone 11: Above 40° F (above 4.5° C)

METRIC CONVERSIONS

U.S. Units to Metric Equivalents			Metric Units to U.S. Equivalents		
To Convert From	Multiply By	To Get	To Convert From	Multiply By	To Get
Inches	25.4	Millimeters	Millimeters	0.0394	Inches
Inches	2.54	Centimeters	Centimeters	0.3937	Inches
Feet	30.48	Centimeters	Centimeters	0.0328	Feet
Feet	0.3048	Meters	Meters	3.2808	Feet
Yards	0.9144	Meters	Meters	1.0936	Yards

To convert from degrees Fahrenheit (F) to degrees Celsius (C), first subtract 32, then multiply by ⁵⁄₉.

To convert from degrees Celsius to degrees Fahrenheit, multiply by ⁹⁄₅, then add 32.

INDEX

A number in boldface indicates
a photograph or illustration.
An asterisk following a number (*)
indicates a descriptive entry in the
"Gallery of Easy Flowers."